Education, Gender and Anxiety

Feminist Perspectives on
The Past and Present
Advisory Editorial Board

Education, Gender and Anxiety

Jenny Shaw

Taylor & Francis
Publishers since 1798

UK   Taylor & Francis Ltd, 4 John St., London WC1N 2ET
USA   Taylor & Francis Inc., 1900 Frost Road, Suite 101, Bristol, PA 19007

First published 1995

A Catalogue Record for this book is available from the British Library

ISBN 0 7484 0101 6
ISBN 0 7484 0102 4 pbk

**Library of Congress Cataloging-in-Publication Data are available on
request**

Typeset in 11/13 pt Times
by Solidus (Bristol) Limited

Printed in Great Britain by SRP Ltd, Exeter.

Contents

Preface

All books have an imaginary reader, a character to whom the argument is addressed. This one has several. On the one hand I imagine a parent, a teacher, an educational administrator or an undergraduate studying sociology, women's studies, or for a BEd or PGCE. Such a reader picks up a book like this because they wish to find a new angle on what has become a fairly familiar topic. But I also nurse the hope that it will be read by therapists, counsellors, depth psychologists or others with clinical experience and a psychoanalytic background; at any rate by those with more experience of 'the inner world' than me, but who may not, routinely, concern themselves with the 'outer world': for the arguments presented here are provisional and need to be confirmed or disconfirmed by data that is only available in the consulting room.

There are, of course, different levels of thinking about gender and the way that sociologists approach the concept, still often through role and status and power, is markedly different from one in which being male or female is regarded as a shifting, confused and partial category. Indeed my imaginary reader, steeped in psychoanalysis and clinical experience, may have no specialist interest in gender at all, and may even be inclined to reject the concept altogether. Still, they may, as part of their daily work, see in greater detail some of the connections that I am trying to draw. If the book is to be of any use it needs those in the position to do so, to say 'Yes, I see that everyday in my work' or, 'No, that is not quite right'. Then, perhaps, a dialogue will grow between gender and education specialists and those with psychoanalytical expertise.

However, perhaps my most fleshed-out 'reader' is a past or present women and education or women's studies MA student at the University of Sussex, most, but not all, of whom were women. Rather like the 'chorus' in Greek tragedy which observes and comments on the action, it was they who had the final say as I struggled to formulate some of these ideas. Did it make sense to these students, most of whom were highly experienced teachers? It was they, and my co-tutor Carol Dyhouse, who enabled me to voice ideas which often seemed off the wall and out of sync with the bulk of literature that we were looking at and, in the end, it is they who I hope to convince with a still incomplete, but somewhat more worked-out argument.

At 6.15 p.m. each Thursday, Carol and I would wonder if we had enough energy to go on, but by nearly 9 p.m. we would end 'high' on the buzz that, each week, the group created. The ideas in this book both come out of those seminar discussions and are inspired by the work produced by the students. When the course started there was not the extensive literature in gender and education that there now is and we used an eclectic set of materials including a lot of life histories. The first essay or assignment was to use such experiential material to explore how much schooling or education had contributed to an understanding of the sexual division of labour. Nearly all the students chose to write about this subject autobiographically, as it seemed easier than an essay based on a lot of texts; soon after starting they realized how daunting such a task can be, and possibly regretted it. Still, year after year, they produced original, thought-provoking and moving essays which uncovered for them, as well as for the rest of the seminar, a rich vein of questions to be answered.

Although M.A. students are obviously not a representative sample, there were a number of recurring themes in the hundred or so autobiographical essays that were produced. One of these was the importance of sibling rivalry and its pains, to a child's growing awareness of gender. Decisions over schooling were often the overt expression of different feelings that parents had about their children; different feelings which would be denied by the claim that all the children were loved and valued equally but explained, if at all, in terms of gender. In families where there were children of each sex this was often expressed in the decision of which, if any, child should receive private schooling, and it was more usually the boy. Another theme was how narcissistic parents can be when making educational decisions for their children. Decisions about the sort of school a child should go to were often made on the basis of the parent's experience at school thirty or forty years earlier, the present child being confused with the parent's memories of his or her childhood. For those who had grown up during, or soon after, the Second World War, there was often a strong sense of an obligation to fulfil certain parental projects which were fairly transparently projected onto the children. Children were often expected to do more than just 'do well' academically and 'get on' as a justification of their parents' sacrifices or as compensation for the War and their past sufferings; they were obliged, especially at school where there was little opportunity for parents to observe what actually went on, to live out their parents' desires and fantasies. As schoolchildren they knew very clearly that they had a 'part' to play, that they had to 'act' being another person and that schooling meant shifting around with voices, identities, personalities. Many of these essays gave clear examples of what it felt like to be the vessel of another person's feelings and this, if nothing else, made me realize why an approach which could conceptualize such processes as projection and introjection had a scope that had hitherto not been fully explored in education.

Most of the themes discussed here were first presented at a conference on Psychoanalysis and the Public Sphere. On that occasion, speaking to therapists, counsellors and psychoanalysts, I was very tentative and aware that, although the conference was focused on the wider application of psychoanalytic ideas, I had no clinical data to offer. I was neither a therapist nor a schoolteacher regularly able to observe children of the relevant age group, although my own children provide me with ample illustration of many common gender differences in relation to schooling. Yet I had taught the sociology of both education and gender for many years and felt reasonably confident in my sense that, although work in this area had expanded, it was also somewhat repetitive and stuck. The general level of discussion needed a change of gear. But, trained in sociology as I was, I was reluctant to venture further without empirical evidence and the opportunity for doing this was not available. It is hard to teach in one institution and observe in another and, whilst some sociologists have trained as analysts or therapists, they have tended to give up sociology. If I was to go on I had to accept the risks of going beyond the usual sociological boundaries and accept that I could only scratch the surface. I have, therefore, used whatever was to hand. The result will no doubt seem eclectic and is inevitably incomplete. Usually, when ideas are taken out of their context and applied elsewhere, there is some ambition to expand their explanatory scope. But my aim is more revisionary; I am not trying to sell psychoanalysis, just to show that there might be a different way of thinking about how gender divisions grow and shift around during the course of formal education.

Many friends have patiently listened to my anxieties about education, gender and this book. I thank them all, especially Carole Satyamurti, Carol Dyhouse, Wenda Bradley, Elizabeth Mestheneos, Jim and Susan Douglas, Mary Barnett, Lizzie Millar, Pat Owen and Andrew Samuels.

Chapter 1

Introduction: The Unconscious Curriculum

As a broad topic, the issue of gender in education is both more or less publicly accepted and widely assumed to be on the wane; at least insofar as talking about gender has meant talking about the educational fortunes of women and girls. Many take the view that though gender in this sense used to be a 'problem', it solved itself once parity in entry and pass rates for GCSE and 'A' level were achieved and men and women entered higher education in roughly equal numbers, as they now do. Indeed, the report from the National Commission on Education *Learning to Succeed* (1993) makes only the briefest mention of gender, and then only in relation to girls and computing. The work begun by feminists and other educationalists in the 1970s to raise consciousness is, in a sense, complete.

The debates about how gender undermines educational opportunities which are theoretically equal, how segmented labour markets influence school practices and outcomes, how teachers discriminate, often inadvertently, and how the all-pervasive discourses of femininity and masculinity shape school experience are more or less over, or at least have come to a halt. It can seem almost old-fashioned to argue that there are still gender issues in education to be taken seriously unless, of course, they are presented as being about boys' declining performance. Stressing the lead that girls now have in reading, in GCSEs and even in 'A' levels, two *Sunday Times* journalists, writing in 1994, claimed 'It is the pitiful performance by boys that now requires radical rethinking to equal opportunities. The question is: have girls had it too good for too long while society has complacently accepted that boys will be boys?' (Hymas and Cohen, 1994).

Catching up in the university entrance stakes is hardly having it 'too good for too long', but it would be perverse to ignore or deny that improvements have occurred. Many of the institutional barriers which once prevented girls and women from receiving the same educational opportunities as boys and men have clearly been removed. Blatant discrimination, such as the rules which once prevented women from taking their degrees at Oxford and Cambridge, the infamous marriage bar for women teachers, or a curriculum system that shunted girls into domestic science and boys into metalwork, have gone. Even where no formal barrier existed there had been informal processes which effectively designated some subjects, such as mathematics and the natural sciences, as male domains in which women and girls were not welcome, or much at home. This has changed, though possibly not as much in physics as in chemistry and biology; but it has changed nevertheless. The natural sciences have become more attractive, or less formidable, to girls. But something else, other than the formal and informal arrangements, manages to produce lines of demarcation every bit as effective as the old ones; this demonstrates that the 'problem' of gender in education is not solved once women and girls' access to certain institutions is improved. That something else is, until it is better understood, pretty invisible and mysterious. It is also mobile, flexible or perhaps opportunistic for, like infections, it finds new environmental niches in which to flourish, for example, computer studies or postgraduate education. Gender divisions in education have not gone away; though they have to some extent gone underground, they flourish in the face of considerable effort to suppress them. But as a going, public concern they have changed, to become less a concern with the fate of girls exclusively and more one of genuinely understanding the interplay between how gender is socially constructed and how schooling adds to, or detracts from, this process.

Girls still seem to take to reading more easily than boys and boys, systematically, get more help to overcome their gender-specific disadvantage. Men teachers in the primary sector have a one-in-two chance of being a deputy or a head, whilst in the secondary school sector there have actually been fewer headships for women since schools became predominantly coeducational. The numbers of women students getting first class degrees at Oxbridge has also declined since the all-women colleges admitted men and, as first degrees lose their 'positional' advantage, postgraduate qualifications have become more critical, but also more male-dominated. And, perhaps most important of all, the arts/science divide which runs along gender lines seems as robust as ever. Lastly, there are gender differences in the impact that education has on later careers. However egalitarian or meritocratic education aims to be, it does not improve the life chances of girls to anything like the extent that it ought to or does, sometimes, for boys. Hardly any of this happens because of overt discrimination, but it happens.

In broad terms girls may be getting as 'good' an education as boys, but this does not secure for them the same lifetime advantages or occupational benefits that it does for men. In a striking study of progress and promotion within the British Civil Service, an organization with a formal commitment to equality of opportunity and meritocracy, Ronald Roberts *et al.* (1993) showed that men did not need their higher educational qualifications to get on and that women, even when they had them, could not profit from them. Of course, occupational mobility is not the same as education, although it is meant, in some degree, to follow from it. Research such as this, which shows how little difference getting a good education may make to women and their careers, how resistant the 'glass ceiling' is to cracking (Gregg and Machin, 1993) and how the percentage of women getting into senior managerial jobs may now be declining, undermines a widely held complacency that assumes improving access to education is an adequate way of achieving social justice and an easy means of reform. It forces anyone concerned about gender, education and its consequences to reconsider their basic assumptions. For what seems almost inescapable is that informal, interpersonal and inter-actional processes have taken over from formal, gender-based barriers to produce much the same effects. And it is these that need to be at the centre of any new theory of gender and education.

As a result, sociologists of education have shifted their interest away from formal obstacles and towards these informal, interpersonal and interactional processes. It is this movement that has brought them nearer to theories, such as psychoanalysis, which deal with the irrational, with unintended consequences and with unconscious processes. Something similar has gone on in the broader field of sociology. Here, the discipline has finally given up its self-imposed obligation to start all discussions with fairly fixed structures (institutions) and moved, through the debate over function-alism, structuration, system and social integration, towards a greater interest in process. Inevitably sub-fields, like education, echo some of the broader intellectual shifts, but there are specific factors within the field of education. Because the sociology of education has always had a strong practical orientation (it is hard to venture the merest idea without being confronted with the question of what should be done, or what policies should be proposed) the whole domain has not dissolved in a flux of postmodernist uncertainty. The basic questions remain: how do educational systems, generate, reinforce or alter gender divisions and what, if anything, should be done? In attempting to answer these questions it is clear that it is individuals, pupils, teachers, parents and administrators who have to make decisions and choices. As subjects, they may be partially created by the institutions in and through which they live, but they maintain a degree of physical substance or materiality which is independent of those institutions. The crucial feature of schooling is that all those who enter do not come out the same. It is individuals who have to negotiate identities and pathways, but what they have to negotiate are educational institutions.

The broad paradigm breakdown in the sociology of education began when ethnicity and gender dislodged class as the main theme and the effects of this have made the whole field less traditionally sociological. One of the most cited of all books in the sociology of education is Paul Willis' *Learning to Labour* (1977), an ethnographic account of twelve young lads in the British midlands who, at the time of the study, could look forward to jobs in the car and other manufacturing industries of the region. Though still at school, their attention and behaviour was largely focused on the class-based culture of the shop floor. And, anticipating their workplace identities, they rejected what the schools had to offer and ridiculed those pupils who took their education seriously. Though they were proud of themselves and their 'resistance', which included a macho attitude to women and a lot of bravado, they were nevertheless securing for themselves a lifetime of subordination and, for a regular supply of labour 'capital'. This, anyway, was the interpretation offered by Willis and was intended to show how sophisticated and devious cultural hegemony could be. Yet today the study is largely remembered as a key, early text in the study of masculinity and macho culture and for illustrating E.P. Thompson's (1963) definition of class as a relationship and not a thing, 'something which happens in human relationships'. Gradually, even those still obsessed with the primacy of class turned to seeing it as a matter of process and interpersonal behaviour.

However, the interpersonal/interactional/culture focus has done more than add a nail to the coffin of class as the backbone of the sociology of education: it has demonstrated the need for a theory, or theories, which encompass or articulate individual and institutional processes. Individualism has long been the bottom line of education, indeed it has been blamed for most of the faults of the British system (Hargreaves, 1980), especially for its capacity to occlude a public perception of education as a 'social good' needing public investment and collective support. This individualism continues to be evident in, and indeed to justify, many recent reforms such as the Assisted Places scheme, the introduction of grant-maintained schools and the City Technology Colleges programme. So agency, individuals, and how they make choices has to be part of the story, but agency need not only be conscious, although it is usually understood as such: it can be semi-conscious or unconscious. And it is this semi-conscious or unconscious agency that gives a new twist to the old idea of the 'hidden curriculum' (Jackson, 1968).

Usually understood as all the social messages which are learned in school, but are most definitely not part of the formal curriculum, the term 'hidden curriculum' is as ubiquitous as it is imprecise. Nevertheless, it gave a huge boost to the study of gender and education because it legitimized and brought together discussion of subtle, covert and often somewhat intangible processes and gave them a unitary name that was not simple 'prejudice'. It was not as clear-cut or as institutionalized a concept as the 'formal curriculum', with which it was paired, but it marked out a territory in which the study of gender and classroom practice or school organization could be undertaken. Throughout the late 1970s and 1980s it was, in fact, the main intellectual paradigm for the sociology of gender and education. Marxist ideas of social reproduction had re-energized the sociology of education in the early part of this period, especially through the work of Sam Bowles and Herb Gintis (1976), but had been notably unable to account for gender; though some socialist feminists such as Michele Barrett (1980) claimed that occupational divisions were the basis of gender divisions in education. But, in general, labour market determinism could neither overcome the fact that girls' academic performance was often as good as, or even better than, that of boys whilst their occupational fortunes were almost always worse, nor the failure to explain exactly how the labour market exerted an influence on educational institutions.

The absence of 'grand' or even 'middle range' theory, plus the difficulty of getting funding, meant that most of the research in this period was empirical, small-scale, qualitative and observation-based. It produced work sensitive to nuance and to group dynamics which was good at showing how far practice diverged from the rhetoric of equal opportunities. It identified how early a form of gender bullying or sexual harassment started in schools and colleges, and how pervasive it was. And it also demonstrated how texts and teaching materials were unwittingly prescriptive and proscriptive about gender, knowledge and status. All of this huddled under the blanket term 'hidden curriculum' which became a shorthand for the informal, the mysterious and the unknown.

All of this was happening in the university seminar. In INSET (in-service training) courses a slightly different tack was taken. Equal access (which focuses on individuals) to all courses, or educational institutions, had been shown to be an insufficient condition for changing gendered outcomes within education and much more concern was gradually given to sexism, to sexual harassment, to discrimination and to 'inner' factors such as identity formation. As awareness of racism and sexism grew, the 'problems' of gender or ethnicity changed from the task of convincing local authorities, schools or colleges to adopt policies and the practice of equal opportunities towards that of combating racism or sexism directly: that is, of getting children, teachers and parents to be less sexist. Much of this work is sensitive to unconscious determinants (Cohen, 1989). Going along with this change has been a certain pessimism, for whilst educational change is always slower than expected, change that is aimed at attitudes tends to be even slower than that which targets rules and regulations. Moreover, gender divisions have the annoying habit of mutating. Just when it seems that progress is being made, such as making science less 'masculine', new fields such as computer studies appear, which are deemed just as socially important, and quickly become predominantly male domains. Thus theories were needed which explained resistance to change as much as the initial emergence of sexual division and this, too, pointed in the direction of psychoanalysis.

However, psychoanalysis is not a panacea. It is not a general theory of gender and education and it does not displace or demolish all other theories. There are many topics about which it is not illuminating, and many of these are educational. But there are some which really can be turned around by the perspective. My grasp of what university seminars are really about and why so many of them are really unpleasant affairs with people leaving feeling anxious, bored, disappointed or, if they were giving a paper, frightened and maybe inadequate, changed fundamentally after reading Roger Holmes' (1967) description of them as re-enacted versions of the primal horde. Freud had used the myth of the primal horde to explain his account of the birth of society and the human capacity to form and maintain groups. It was a psychological version of the 'social contract' theory and in it the collective guilt at real or symbolic patricide played a large part. Shared guilt, as much as mutual fear, tempered the individual aspirations and jealousies and led to the invention of rules, morality and social institutions which could contain and channel potential aggression.

Holmes took the argument out of pre-history and applied it to all ritualized and formal meetings, of which the university seminar was just an example. The chairman, the room plan and the behaviour of participants were analysed in terms of power, predictability and control. The chairman was simultaneously omnipotent and impotent, he was ultra-real and powerful, yet non-existent; he could not talk. He was treated with exaggerated awe and deference. When the audience came in they chose, voluntarily, to sit in particular places, most notably not in the front seats, and when they spoke they did so in a form of coded aggression and sarcasm. At some level, everyone in the seminar wants to dispossess the speaker and is inhibited only by fear of retaliation from the speaker and revenge from other, disappointed, seminar members who entertain similar ambitions. Hence the rituals of speaking to the 'chair' are accepted and votes of thanks given to the most boring of speakers. In this account, Holmes used a psychoanalytical vocabulary to describe the behaviour in an educational setting that was, at least for me, very familiar and convincing.

Psychoanalysis is a theory of meaning and of symbols; it is open-ended, not final. It aims to provoke and stimulate, to lead to another train of ideas. A recent justification of it as a way of telling stories praises the ambiguity of psychoanalysis for returning the reader to his or her thoughts.

> Psychoanalysis – as a form of conversation – is only worth having if it makes our lives more interesting, or funnier, or sadder, or more tormented – or whatever it is about ourselves that we value and want to promote; and especially if it helps us to find new things about ourselves that we didn't know we could value. (Phillips, 1993, p. xvii)

This book was originally intended to apply three or so well known psychoanalytical concepts or papers to three or four rather intractable school-based problems: just to show that there was another way of approaching gender differences in reading and writing, classroom interaction, sex-stereotyped subject choice and the single-sex/coeducation school debate. At first I simply wanted to introduce into an educational context the ideas of social systems as defences against anxiety, of certain aspects of learning as being based on feeding, of the different implications for each sex of separation from their mothers and of school subjects or disciplines as functioning as 'transitional objects'. I never imagined that this would lead to a general theory of gender and education and, because I had no original data to present, I envisaged a fairly speculative attempt to re-open a discussion that had become rather stuck and predictable. There seemed to be some scope for such an attempt because, for a variety of reasons, the discourses of education and psychoanalysis had been unusually well insulated from each other.

As time passed two processes converged. First, I began to realize that there was a common theme to the set of psychoanalytic papers I wanted to use and that this lay in individual, or institutional, responses to anxiety. The second was that as the changes introduced to the British education system by the 1989 Education Reform Act began to be visible, I saw that it might even be possible to make a prediction. This is still a fairly unusual thing to do in the social sciences, but I was moving towards a view of gender divisions within education as a sort of collective defence mechanism. As a central tenet of psychoanalytic thought is that defence mechanisms are triggered by anxiety, I realized that there was at least a possibility of suggesting that if general levels of anxiety within an education system were raised, as I think they are with all the testing and change that has occurred, then we might expect, or predict, a deepening of gender divisions within them. At the moment this is still speculation. To take it further, more time and detailed empirical research is needed. At this stage all that I can hope to do is spell out why certain gender divisions in education are tied to anxiety.

I hope that it is clear that I am not turning to psychoanalysis because of a diffuse sense that there is a theoretical vacuum at the heart of the gender and education debate and that psychoanalysis could fill it. Whilst I believe that there is mileage to be gained from applying the perspective to the expressions of gender that appear in educational settings, I am not suggesting that psychoanalysis will plug all the gaps in knowledge or solve all the practical problems. I am not a psychoanalyst and my choice of texts and ideas is skimpy to say the least. I use those which have struck me as being applicable to a range of gender 'problems' in education that I happen to think are the most serious in their social consequences. Obviously there are other issues, perhaps just as important, which will not be amenable to a psychoanalytic or depth psychology approach in any shape or form. I certainly do not intend to champion a psychoanalytic or depth psychology approach above all others.

At this stage, I am not proposing a comprehensive theory of gender in education, though there is a clear implication that if sexual divisions in education act as a defence against educationally produced anxiety then we can be reasonably sure that, as anxiety increases, so will sexual divisions, in a variety of forms. Certainly, the grounds for thinking this way are strengthened as the levels of public anxiety about education in Great Britain are increased with more formal testing points, the publication of league tables and worry about the future of schools, in or outside of Local Education Authority control. The central argument of this book which, I think, justifies importing psychoanalytical ideas, is that anxiety is central to the functioning of education systems and to the form that gender takes within them. It seems unlikely that formal education could have no effect on the formation of gender identities, but exactly how is still a mystery unless, as I shall try to show, we look at the role of anxiety and responses to it.

I am acutely aware of the tendency for 'theory' and 'practice' to diverge, for theory to become little more than intellectual history and to lose touch with any sort of application. In this case, although I argue that part of the value of a psychoanalytic approach is its perspective on the inner obstacles to change, it is as much the continuing demand for suggestions on 'what to do about gender in education' that persuades me to take this direction. As a whole tier of educational organization (the Local Educational Authority) is dismantled, so too is the potential for reform which was once vested in it. The notion of collective interests, and the means for protecting them, as well as the duty to take note of professional expertise and plan education, are being diminished.

Although it is long time since one did, a LEA could decide to open or retain a single-sex school because of community needs. However, once the overall planning structure is removed and a different set of mechanisms, loosely related to 'markets' and individuals, take over it cannot; and the picture around gender must change. Paradoxically, though league tables consistently show how well independent girls' schools do (the first eleven of the schools with the best GCSE results in a 1994 *Sunday Times* survey), the independent, i.e. market, sector is not opening new girls' schools any more than is the state sector. The decline of single-sex schools may have halted, but this sort of education is still an option for only a minority. There is thus an urgent need for theories which explain how gender is developed within the processes of interaction between the sexes, for concerted action may well be restricted to this level. The removal of the means of representing collective interests, or guarding those who might not be able to energetically represent themselves or buy what they want, means that processes at the personal and small group level become stronger and more critical: their scope is widened once one means of combating them is reduced.

It may not require too much imagination to see anxiety as a secret weapon, or rather a technique of educational management, when it takes the form of examinations for pupils and appraisal and performance-related pay for staff; but it might be harder to see how broad gender divisions in schools may also be explained in this way. The answer, though, comes through in a series of specific issues or problems. These are: the pattern of girls' and boys' reading (mainly in the early years at primary school, but to some extent later on too), the sex-stereotyped and polarized subject choices that characterize secondary and higher education, and the debate about coeducation or single-sex schools. In each case I try to show how a psychoanalytic paper, though not written for an educationalist audience, might revise standard interpretations of what is going on.

Meanwhile, other shifts in educational thought and political philosophy have gathered pace. Simple notions of equality have receded and it has became more important to think about equity and what sort of differences are compatible with it. In this respect all the issues that I am concerned with, single-sex versus coeducational schools, subject stereotyping and polarization, reading habits and classroom interaction, pose intriguing problems. These include whether gender divisions should always be challenged and/or reduced, and the resource implications of 'accepting' some differences such as those which appear in maths but attempting to remedy others such as those which appear as reading difficulties or 'low self-esteem'. I am convinced that differences in reading aptitude and in subject choice will remain important sources of gender division and resource allocation, the introduction of a national curriculum and testing notwithstanding. And, though I could not have anticipated quite how much of a fillip the provision for grant-maintained schools or the introduction of league tables would give to single-sex schooling, I have been less ready than some of my colleagues to think that the debate about coeducational schooling is dead. Single-sex schools may be a good example of where difference rather than equality can lead to equity.

Concerned teachers, as well as concerned parents, want to know what they can or should do about children giving up subjects that they like because they would rather be with their friends. They want to know what to do if, despite a commitment to equal opportunities, they find themselves giving more time and attention to boys; or what to do about boys who harass girls. They need to consider the tricky arguments for, perhaps, supporting a school that wants to opt out in order to stay single-sex, remain comprehensive, or start on the road to becoming selective. Parents have often to weigh up the interests of their sons against those of their daughters. There are no easy answers to any of these questions, and often some sort of answers are needed long before research can be done. Meanwhile, the arguments go on. Psychoanalysis is not a quick fix to any of these issues but it allows us to come at them in a slightly different way.

If I have an agenda for teachers, parents and administrators, it is that some gender differences should not necessarily be eliminated and that not all are equally pernicious or disturbing. If we are clearer about what is causing them we may use our very limited powers of intervention more effectively. Education until 16 is compulsory and it is for this reason that reformers eye it so keenly as the royal route to social change. What happens in school is expected to have a profound effect, and it tends to, but not always exactly as expected. Politicians, in their cross-party enthusiasm for standards and testing, should note that they have negative consequences too and start worrying about them. As with coeducational schooling, something that looks like a good idea may well work our rather differently.

This book is organized around five broadly interconnected themes, all of which are linked by the idea that defences against anxiety create the preconditions for gender differentiation. There is an even deeper commitment, though, to the idea that the capacity to learn is influenced by stages in psychosexual developmental stages and that, as Meltzer (1973) says, the educational cycle ignores this at pupils' peril. Although I deal with reading before subject choice and it is implicit that problems at the early reading stage might be related to Oedipal conflicts, whilst those that appear in secondary schools are connected with puberty and adolescence, I have not tried to make a developmental case. My sense of the outstanding problems in education precede my hunch that a psychoanalytical approach might help solve them and each chapter started off simply as the application of a particular paper or concept to a gender-related problem in schooling.

The first and most general theme is that unconscious processes and anxiety affect learning. To illustrate it I take reading and writing and start with a paper on the unconscious determinants of reading written in 1930 by James Strachey. Reading is the first organized activity of formal schooling. It is, psychologically and socially, heavily loaded and built into measures of ability, i.e. reading ages. The perceived success and failure of teachers, of primary schools and of children depend upon it. Yet not all children swiftly become happy and proficient readers and a gender difference in reading is one of the most striking in the early stages of schooling. Though some reading is learned in the one-to-one situation of a parent and child, much of it takes place within the context of a classroom: in both settings there are unconscious factors affecting progress as well as conscious and social ones. Of course, if we accept that behaviour is, in varying degrees, affected by forces of which we are not aware, then the impact of unconscious ideas, fantasies and fears will be far greater than just on how we learn to read. They will, as I think they do, also affect the subjects we choose, our relations with teachers and other pupils, and how we behave in groups.

The second general theme is crystallized in the idea that teachers are not only legally but emotionally 'in loco parentis'. There are probably few children who have not slipped and at some time called their teacher 'Mummy' or their mother 'Miss'. Teaching is not the same as parenting, but it depends upon it in a wide variety of ways, both practically and emotionally. In particular it is the primitive, primary and practical experience of feeding and being fed that lays the foundations for learning in general. As being fed is something that parents, and mothers especially, do, it not only forms the basis for learning (ingesting), but a strong sense of gender and gender-appropriate relations are inscribed into that early experience. It is, then, not surprising that the sexual divisions around parenting are easily transferred into sexual divisions around teaching and learning. The parent/child relation is the imprimatur of all later relations and elaborating this is, of course, one of the central insights of psychoanalysis.

The third theme stems from the first two, and explores how far school 'subjects' such as maths, english and science can be compared to the 'transitional objects' that Donald Winnicott (1953, 1971) accorded such importance to in infancy. Moments of anxiety occur throughout life and our ways of dealing with them become more sophisticated, but the early experiences of maternal failure which we all experience, and have to find a solution to, lay the ground for the later strategies. When Winnicott was elaborating his theory of the 'transitional object' his primary concern was to explain how infants grew apart from their mothers without totally falling apart. He saw that the favourite toy, teddy bear or blanket was not only important as a substitute for what was really wanted (a re-establishment of the relationship with whoever it was that mainly looked after the child and met his or her needs) and as a solace, it was the prototype way of coping alone and, more importantly, was an essential stage and means for developing as an autonomous individual.

Though school subjects may not, at first, seem like a teddy bear, there is a lot of 'playing safe' and avoiding risk in their choosing. In chapters 6 and 7, I elaborate a parallel in the psychological experiences of infancy and adolescence and in the strategies of dealing with them which culminate in the sex-stereotyped subject choice that has become a 'problem' in education. The argument is basically that subjects or disciplines are symbols of both people and a relationship and that, when pressure or anxiety is placed on a pupil by the demand that they choose a subject and face up to impending examinations or to life as an adult, *and teaching changes from being person-based, as it is in primary schools, to being subject-based, as it is in secondary schools*, academic subjects then acquire a particular importance. Undoubtedly, the fact that subjects are perceived as 'masculine' or 'feminine' is a social construction, but constructionist or cultural theories (unless they are behaviourist at root and depend on the theory of positive and negative reinforcement) do not explain why any social definition or construction is accepted and conformed to, especially in an era where there is much self-consciousness and effort to change them.

The fourth theme is the gender dynamics of groups. Everyone knows that schools are about more than just formal learning. They have a social dimension too. Friendships are made and broken all the time and teachers accommodate to this by exploiting or interrupting friendships as they see fit. Informally there is much single-sex setting, just as there is covert setting by ability and, occasionally, this is deliberately engineered or prevented. Often it is just given in to. Mixed-sex groups can be more trouble than they are worth to the harassed teacher, especially as children get older. Subcultures, of which the spontaneous single-sex sets are a part, form an important subversive role in education. They exist precisely to undermine something or someone. Teachers know this and often fear the loss of their control as well as the greater potential for delinquency that is widely assumed to accompany subcultures.

It is easy to paint a picture of the overt task of schooling continuously being undermined by, or threatened with being undermined by, a potent subculture, but there is probably not a domestic science teacher in the land who does not have a story of bread making with boys, all of whom seem quick to perceive the phallic potential of dough. Wilfrid Bion's (1961) work on experiences in groups does not directly address gender divisions and dynamics but his model of groups as being formed around the tension between the overt or formal task and another more primitive 'basic assumption' which group members periodically share and use for unconscious psychic purposes is relevant. The three archetypical 'basic assumption' groups that he describes are all inspired by, or derived from, early experiences of being parented and it is in these that the seeds of later gender identities can be found.

For most of us schools are the most coercive institutions that we ever experience. It is the only time of our lives when we are legally compelled to be somewhere and do something: as a result, we are least in control of our destiny. This can lead to an overestimation of the influence of schools. Whatever their long-term effects (and there is considerable controversy over how long lasting any of the effects of schooling might be in terms of earnings or occupation) it may not be the distinctive characteristics of educational institutions that have an effect. The technologies of testing and assessment, the curriculum, the legal compulsion to attend and the method of organizing time may pale beside the essential nature of schools as predicated upon and embodying quasi-family rules and relations. In later chapters I argue that it is the covert use of parenting that effectively imports gender into schooling and keeps it there through the emotions that are attached to parents and their substitutes. I also suggest that the most common understanding of gender, as a social construction only loosely and contingently based on sex, may be too abstract for the educational context. Whilst we promote 'gender' as a unitary concept to carve out a space for social process and to avoid charges of essentialism and biologism, we may find that terms like femininity and masculinity become rather ideological and get stranded away from any sense of social practice. In schools and colleges the experiences that matter are those that get incorporated and tied up with prior experiences of *mothers* and *fathers* and, later, of *siblings* too.

The fifth theme, that of the role of anxiety in education, is where I actually start, for it underpins the whole project. I argue that if we look at where gender becomes a problem in educational terms we can see that it is most acute where anxiety is greatest and that these gender differences may themselves be part of a response to that anxiety. Of course, some readers may find any argument couched in terms of anxiety too all-embracing, especially as anxiety is not easy to distinguish from fear. Sarason and his colleagues, when writing about anxiety among elementary school children, defined it as 'a relationship between a present danger and unconscious but, concurrently active, contents and processes deriving from previously unresolved conflicts' (Sarason *et al.*, 1960, p. 6). Like most psychiatrically based definitions this one stressed that the roots of anxiety lay in early relationships and does not leave much room for other sources. However, anxiety is multi-casual and although most causes might lie in an individual's biography, some will be produced directly by social settings such as interviews, examinations and selection. As we are all capable of anxiety it is not difficult to accept that school conventions might exploit and/or promote it. What is less obvious, but possibly just as important, is how educationally produced anxiety and institutionalized defences against it combine to produce sexual divisions in schooling.

The idea that social formations may arise as a result of acute anxiety and develop in ways that provide members of a community with a means of psychic defence is commonplace amongst psychoanalysts and has been described in detail by Isabel Menzies Lyth (1959). It provides a bridge between psychoanalysis and sociology, or the sociology of education, precisely because educational institutions both produce anxiety and shape the way individuals deal with it. However, at this stage, I only want to establish a superficial relationship between where gender arises as a problem in the educational context and general levels of anxiety. Anxiety, of course, can have many causes, but it is the ones that are integral to educational institutions that I am concerned with.

I do not go thoroughly into theoretical differences and divisions within psychoanalysis, and will often appear to ride roughshod over distinctions which others may regard as fundamental. Nor do I deal with similar differences within feminism. My aim is to stay grounded in the school-based problems and to take, eclectically, whatever might be usefully applied to them. Many of the ideas I discuss are associated with the psychoanalysts know as the 'independents' or with the term 'object relations'. However I did not start out with an allegiance to this group or this 'school', only a sense that the most pressing problems left in the gender and education debate were sex differences in reading and writing, gendered patterns of classroom inter-action, subject polarization at the secondary school and higher education level and the paradoxical treatment or reputation of coeducational and single-sex schooling. In many of these areas research had come to a stop. Projects on single-sex/coeducational schooling were not getting funded, gender differences around reading invariably got tied up with debates about whether dyslexia really existed or about 'real books' versus 'reading schemes' as methods of teaching reading. The issue of subject choice had got confined to girls and science rather than to gender more broadly as a determinant of choice and, as girls began to catch up in some areas and even overtake boys, the liberal assumption of self-sustaining progress re-appeared as a justifica-tion for putting gender on the back burner. Worrying counter trends, such as those in computing studies where gender divisions were increasing, were left to IT specialists and sidelined.

In the last fifteen or so years, since the demise of functionalist and reproductionist theories of education, sociologists and feminists have drawn a picture of gender in education but not really explained it, except insofar as they have relied on the term 'hidden curriculum'. Yet, hiding behind the hidden curriculum, rather like the 'Windows' software package which I used when writing this book, is an unconscious curriculum. The reasons why some children, boys especially, are slow or reluctant readers is largely due to unconscious conflicts, and their adaptations or solutions to these conflicts affect much of their later patterns of learning and subject choice. A good part of the reason that girls thrive more in primary than in secondary schools is also because of their unconscious identifications with women teachers. And the way that the heated debate about single-sex or coeducational schooling is conducted owes far more to unconscious or semi-conscious fears and anxieties than to empirical evidence.

There are several reasons for thinking that psychoanalytic ideas might be relevant to issues of education and gender. First, there has been a general shift of interest away from formal, conscious and visible discrimination towards the informal which leads, pretty quickly, to the invisible and the unconscious. Second, the variable, mutating and fluid nature of gender divisions within education demands a theory that can take account of resistances and transformation (though not everything has changed and quite often what does change tends to be of decreasing importance). Third, psychoanalytic theory is especially suited to social settings where the parenting motif is profound and is fundamentally incorporated in institutional arrangements. Fourth, anxiety-making situations are part and parcel of the social technology of teaching, most notably testing and examinations, and psychoanalysis is largely the theory of how people deal with anxiety. The final and most obvious reason is that the most important symbolic form of gender in education, the division into arts and sciences of girls and boys, probably has the deepest long-term consequences.

In a way this whole book is a response to a challenge thrown up by John Pratt (1984) who thought that what was missing in the research on sex-stereotyping and subject choice was an account of the mechanisms of polarization. It aims to show that there is such an account and that it can be found within the psychoanalytical theory known as 'object relations'. Hence the first half of the book prepares the ground for taking up this challenge by showing why object relations theory is relevant to matters of gender and education and the second half illustrates it.

Chapter 2

Education, Sociology and Feminism: Themes and Perspectives and Object Relations

The way any field develops is partly a matter of serendipity, partly politics, fashion and funding and partly the impact of teaching. Gender and education is no exception. It is a three-cornered speciality squeezed in between education, sociology and feminism which has to relate to a trio of theoretical perspectives. The last chapter suggested that a decade or more of research had slowly but surely shown that what mainly needed to be done was to identify and analyse informal processes and interpersonal behaviour: in the course of this the search for useful theory had shifted in the direction of psychoanalysis.

However, psychoanalysis is still often seen as a quasi-academic discipline, profound maybe and increasingly legitimized by university courses, but still somewhat out on a limb. Though influential in some subjects such as literature, feminism and even parts of sociology, there are other areas where its impact has been negligible, and education is one of these. It would obviously take much more than a short chapter to cover the history of the theoretical, epistemological and political disputes that have characterized the course of psychoanalytical influence in any of the areas, let alone all three. Instead, the purpose of this chapter is, in the first place, to explore why sociology, education and feminism have responded differently to psycho-analytical ideas and then to describe in more detail the 'object relations' school where interest amongst social scientists has converged. The tale in each field is rather different: it is not a case of an intellectual fashion sweeping all before it, except in the sense that the rising interest in gender has profoundly affected most of the humanities and social sciences and made the study of interpersonal processes more central in all of them.

Education

Despite a widespread feeling that the sociology of education has been dominated in recent years by studies of gender and race, as an analytical category gender has made rather little impact on mainstream educational theory. It is treated as an 'add-on' or a specialist interest and, despite the admirable work of a number of feminist researchers (Kanter, 1977; Shakeshaft, 1987; Blackmore and Kenway, 1993) most organizational theory used within education remains untouched. Though gender clearly influences the hidden and the formal curriculum, the teaching process and the nature of educational or administrative hierarchies, the preoccupation of the whole field with understanding schools as organizations and with identifying organizational imperatives has led to a level of abstraction that renders gender a trivial detail. For some time whilst attention was given to the curriculum (Whlyd, 1983) and the different career tracks of men and women teachers (Acker, 1989; de Lyon and Mignoulo, 1989; Ozga, 1988; Connell, 1985), the patriarchal root assumptions of educational bureaucracies went relatively unquestioned (though see Blackmore, 1993).

The reproductionist, or marxist, models which were once widely used in the sociology of education had a fairly short heyday and were widely criticized for their failure to explain gender divisions. For a while it was argued that segregated labour markets governed gendered educational processes and outcomes (Barrett, 1980), though quite how was never explained. Once female educational outcomes improved (without a corresponding improvement in female labour market prospects), this approach faded away. With the collapse of marxism fairly generally and the need to understand why that happened, there was a general turning inward in theory-building and feminists, along with other leftward leaning theorists, began to make tracks towards psychoanalysis, as much as anything to explain resistance to change, collusion and self-subordination (Lasch, 1981).

In mainstream educational theory the course has been somewhat different. At the macro level it has a distinctly pragmatic, managerial rationale and is concerned with systems, organization, outcomes, performance and the curriculum. Here the absence of psychoanalytic ideas, except in the form of a certain sort of management consultancy associated with the Tavistock and Grubb Institutes and the work of Elizabeth Richardson (1967, 1973) is unsurprising. Although the organizational literature has toyed with ideas about how sexuality might be embedded as a central principle (Hearn and Parkin, 1987; Hearn *et al.*, 1989) this has hardly affected education. Somewhat more surprising is the absence of interest in that branch of sociology of education concerned with gender, given that feminism has generally been quite open to psychoanalytical ideas. The reasons for this are various and undoubtedly relate to varieties of feminism and varieties of psychoanalysis; but there are some other, more local, reasons why psycho-analysis has made little impact on educational thinking.

In the first place, a child-centred primary school pedagogy has prevailed which, as Barbara Lloyd and Gerard Duveen (1992) comment, failed to theorize sexuality and intergroup relations in schools and 'naturalized' all discussion of sex as gender. The accompanying ideology of childhood innocence has thus blinded educationalists to the consequences of sex differences, including that of the gender difference in reading which is taken up in chapter 5. In the second place, the resistance to psychoanalytical ideas in education is clearly linked to their association with 'Special Education' – the field with the 'lowest' status in education. As theoretical hierarchies tend to follow institutional ones, a wide berth is generally given to Special Education and its intellectual framework, and those keen on establishing or raising their own intellectual credibility tend to distance themselves, consciously or unconsciously, from everything to do with Special Education and its intellectual framework. Psychiatrists working with 'school refusers' or 'school phobic' children freely use psychoanalytical ideas and, indeed, tend to see all reluctance to go to school in terms of attachment, loss and separation anxiety. But it is rare for such insights to be applied to 'normal' children or go beyond the child guidance community. It is part of the equation of psychoanalysis with pathology and deviance.

Sociology

Sociology never wholly turned its back on psychoanalysis, but the history of the relationship is a rather complicated one mediated by a concern with political critique. In the United States, Talcott Parsons used psychoanalytical ideas to explain socialization and how norms function to maintain social institutions (Parsons and Bales, 1964). Charged as being ultra-conservative, functionalism is now taught almost only as an example of how not to theorize about society and, because of its association with functionalism and Parsons, the psychoanalytically inspired part of his argument has been jettisoned along with the rest. A similar, conservative-leaning, tradition can be found both in the systems theory and management consultancy approach of Elliot Jaques (1955) and, in a rather more complex way, in the cultural critiques of American society by Christopher Lasch (1977, 1979). But to associate the use of psychoanalytical ideas for social analysis only with conservative social thought would be wrong. Mass Observation, a radical pre-war exercise in the sociology of everyday life, was strongly influenced by psycho-analytical ideas and was designed to collect material such as dreams and daydreams so that unconscious material could be taken into account in any resulting sociological theory. Influenced by surrealism as much as by ethology, it clearly had subversive aims as part of its hidden agenda, though, like functionalism, it is now largely viewed as one of sociology's wrong turnings. More recently, sociologists such as Michael Rustin (1991), Ian Craib (1989), Barry Richards (1984), Robert Bocock (1976) and the Jungian analyst Andrew Samuels (1993) have paved the way in showing how sociology, politics and psychoanalysis can be synthesized and yet escape instant dismissal as functionalist.

The speciality of the sociology of education, however, has never fully embraced these ideas, though the historian Carolyn Steedman's essay on primary school pedagogy as 'The Mother made Conscious' (1985) and her book *The Tidy House* (1982) show how psychoanalytical ideas might be deployed, as does some of the psychologist Valerie Walkerdine's work (1981, 1990). As suggested in the last chapter, issues of gender entered the sociology of education via a general concern with access to educational opportunity which, though important, was both short-term and unconcerned with the experience once the access is gained. Still, despite the dominance of access, and unlike mainstream sociology, there was another strand in the sociology of education potentially more hospitable to an interest in the inner world. This was the interest in socialization and role theory which had pretty much declined (like functionalism to which it was related) elsewhere in sociology. For, providing role is not understood wholly in behaviourist terms (as a response to a stimulus provided by the social environment), it can lead fairly directly to the psychoanalytical ideas of introjection, projection and projective identification. Extremely popular in the late 1960s, role theory was heavily attacked for being theoretically inadequate (i.e. 'only' descriptive), conservative, ahistorical and incapable of dealing with power; yet, at an everyday level, it survived as a plausible explanation of social character. Some of the criticism levelled at the concept was certainly just: it did not explain how some people escaped from or transformed their roles, why people accepted them in the first place, or the power differences between different roles, and it could be pretty behaviourist. But it was theoretically more interesting than its critics allowed (Coulson, 1980). Socialization theories depended upon role, and role theories depended on some notion of modelling which, in turn, depended on mechanisms such as introjection, projective identification etc. (Connell, 1971).

Thus the limited impact of psychoanalytical ideas on sociology is tied up with prejudice and the fortunes of both functionalism and role theory.

Feminism and the Move towards Psychoanalysis

Despite their popularity with students and the rise of market forces in academia, women's studies and gender studies are still not a sufficiently taken-for-granted part of the curriculum for them to overcome much of the earlier opposition. In many disciplines they remain marginal and are subject to the demand that they justify their existence through the development of a 'proper' body of theory. Though this demand owes more to academic politics than the state of the field (where such a demand is probably premature) it explains the attraction of theories developed elsewhere, especially theories that fudge or are ambiguous about essentialism, such as psychoanalysis. Where courses in women's studies or feminism have an independent existence as departments in their own right the picture changes dramatically. Theory proceeds less defensively and, unlike the outposts in sociology and education, it is centrally interested in the link between the individual and the social structure, social form and personal identity. Thus, feminist sociologists working in the field of education have no difficulty posing questions such as 'Why do men manage and women teach?', 'Why are some subjects masculine or feminine?', 'How does education contribute to the formation of gendered identities?' or 'Why does improved educational performance by girls have so little impact on their educational fortunes and careers?'. But neither feminism in general, nor a feminist sociology of education, has a plausible and singular theory to help answer these questions, though, for external reasons, the pressure to find such a theory has intensified.

The question of how much, if any, of the difference between the sexes is innate and how much is socially constructed, though not the only or even the most important question, still haunts feminist theory. Indeed, avoiding the charge of biological determinism can so distort that almost any discussion of stable differences between men and women risks being seen as essentialist and only a short step from biological determinism (Segal, 1987). Psycho-analysis in its various forms, however, seems to fudge this issue. Male and female elements may still be presented as instinctive and innate, as in Donald Winnicott's (1971) description of maleness as 'active relating' and female-ness as 'passive being related to', but it is done in the context of a theory of a universal bisexuality and with the very clear caveat that these are elements, not persons. Other strands of psychoanalysis, such as the Jungian, also stress a gender difference (as animus and anima) but, again, expect them to coexist in everyone. Because this sort of approach does not insist that gender differences are biologically fixed, but rather that gender is fluid or perhaps not even very important at all, psychoanalysis is one of the friendlier intellectual environments in which feminists and sociologists can go fishing. And, after an initial stand-off period, feminists were amongst the most enthusiastic borrowers of psychoanalytic concepts.

This turn-around was largely the result of the work of Juliet Mitchell. Her *Psychoanalysis and Feminism* (1974) stemmed the tide of dismissiveness and challenged the assumption that Freud was a simple, conservative patriarch whose thought could have no relevance to feminism. A little later she performed a similar role in relation to Lacan (Mitchell and Rose, 1982) who, for a period, was a major influence on feminist theory (despite much of his work being just as easily interpreted as supportive rather than subversive of patriarchy) and for Melanie Klein too (Mitchell, 1986). Since Mitchell broke through the feminist taboo on Freud and challenged the view that psychoanalysis was a conservative scheme to 'normalize' people and make them accept their traditional sex roles, feminists have energetically explored the whole spectrum (Brennan, 1989; Tong, 1989). Because of its stress on the importance of language, many feminists working in literary criticism have found the work of Jaques Lacan and the Ecole Freudienne stimulating whilst others, more often sociologists, have tended to favour 'object relations' or Kleinian versions of psychoanalysis. However, too much can be made of the differences. Both psychoanalysis and feminism are prone to division with 'Lacanians' set against 'object relations theorists' or 'Freudians', both in and outside of feminist debate (Barrett, 1992).

Paradoxically, while many British feminists have turned to France, American feminists similarly interested in psychoanalysis have taken up the British object relations theorists. The most influential of these was Nancy Chodorow, whose *Reproduction of Mothering* (1978) has probably been as important as Mitchell's *Psychoanalysis and Feminism*. Chodorow posed the question of why women continue to accept the role of being a mother when it has such penalties and was so undervalued. The same question had been asked the other way round a decade earlier by her compatriot Margaret Polatnick (1984) who, in a tough polemical piece called 'Why Don't Men Rear Children?', had given the answer as 'power'. If child rearing was prestigious, she argued, men would do it. Chodorow took a different line and, drawing directly on object relations, argued that the answer lay in the differential impact on boys' and girls' emotional development of a pattern of childrearing and socialization which left the care of infants and children of both sexes almost wholly to women, yet demanded that boys grew up and identified with their fathers or other males. Whilst still largely in the care of women, boys were supposed to switch psychological identification to men, with whom they might have rather little direct contact, and separate psychologically from their mothers. Girls, on the other hand, were not required to establish their identity in terms of being different to their mothers, as boys were, so, for them, individuation did not mean psychological separation.

The answer to Chodorow's initial question was that girls never really separated from their mothers, instead they got used to the experience of mutual identification and a sense of mergedness which led them to appear good at 'people work', to choose the caring professions and to accept the role of primary parent. Thus, 'mothering' continued generation after generation. Though Chodorow has been heavily criticized in some quarters and is regarded somewhat as the archetypal 'matricentric' thinker opposed to the 'patricentric' Freudians or Lacanians, the main thrust of her argument is widely accepted and has generated work on mother/daughter relationships such as Terry Apter's (1990) *Altered Loves* which supports the general thesis of a continuing and high degree of identification between mothers and daughters.

The conflict and controversy that followed Chodorow's work can, in part, be seen as an extension of the conflicts that have dogged the psychoanalytical movement, both internally and in its relations with the non-psychoanalytical world (Roazen, 1970). But in the case of feminist theory there is an additional reason for the often exaggerated and artificial sense of division. Academics who largely teach the field tend, for pedagogic reasons, to mould their material into a framework of oppositions. Teaching encourages pigeon-holing, classification and false polarization and, because feminist scholarship has survived mostly within the institutions of higher education, much of its material is formatted in this way. Opposition and exaggeration are pedagogical devices which have become institutionalized, and add to the tendency to fragment that is ever present within any political movement. They have just been carried over into feminist scholarship. This effect of teaching is rarely considered because, in Britain anyway, pedagogy or the theory of teaching is still so underdeveloped (Simon, 1985) and the largely untrained university lecturer is possibly the least reflective teacher of all (Schon, 1983).

However, for all the false polarizations, interest in psychoanalysis has grown steadily though patchily in feminism, sociology and education.

Historians and sociologists, as well as literary and cultural theorists, have adapted and used psychoanalytic ideas (Rustin, 1991; Figlio, 1988; Richards, 1984) and, as postmodernism has ushered in a greater intellectual tolerance, there has been a general move away from broad mechanical models (class in the case of sociology and the Freudian 'id', 'ego' and 'superego' in the case of psychoanalysis). Whilst in feminism the coercive typology which once treated political categories as synonymous with theory and made out that all feminism could be fitted into the schema of radical feminism, socialist or marxist feminism or liberal feminism has weakened. As a result, inter-disciplinary work is much easier.

Psychoanalysis and Sociology

A willingness to accept that unconscious processes exist, even though they cannot be seen, is a fundamental assumption of all psychoanalysis. It is a sort of nominal definition which makes the rest of the explanatory system possible. Evidence for the existence of unconscious processes rests on effects which are visible rather than on processes which have to be inferred. Accidents are perhaps the easiest and most accessible examples. We never mean to shoot across the traffic lights, it is just that we were thinking of something else at the time. Given the shifting nature of most social scientific data it is mainly a matter of choice how much one is prepared to work with material open to multiple and variable interpretations, but it is extraordinarily restricting to simply rule it out. The idea that the only proper object of study for sociology is intentional or 'rational' action has long since gone, indeed the discipline is now predominantly concerned with the unintended con-sequences of human action and its unexpected outcomes. As this redefinition gathered pace it was inevitable that the best worked out theory of the irrational, psychoanalysis, should be rehabilitated.

The model of the mind originally described by Freud was a structural, almost mechanical one, consisting of the 'id', 'ego' and 'superego'. The 'id' stood for a basic life force, a bundle of impulses derived from biological needs that provided the momentum for physical and psychological development. The 'ego' was a construct very close to the common-sense understanding of 'self'. It was a vehicle for containing and organizing the raw impulses in ways that served the individual's interests and purposes. As a form of psychological organization it had to be achieved and it did not come 'naturally'. The 'superego' acted as a check on the ego; though an internal construct, it represented the interests of others, of society more generally and is usually understood as a sort of 'conscience'. The ego kept the id in check and the superego did the same for the ego. This equilibrium-based model is not as widely accepted as it once was, and most psychoanalysts now place more importance on interpersonal relations; nevertheless, the potency accorded to the irrational, in the form of the id or the unconscious more generally, has not been diminished. More recent interpretations, whether Jungian, Kleinian or 'middle group', however, are distinguished by a belief that the mind, the heart and the psyche are forged in the process of relating to other people. Overall this has led both to a more holistic approach than classical Freudianism and to more stress on infant relations with the mother.

Freud's ultimate objective had been neurological; thus, though he listened to the material that his patients brought him about their families and was intent on decoding their unconscious and fantasy-laden meanings, his aetiological aim had been, and remained, a reductionist one which led him inwards to the brain and not outwards to other people. This overrode and, perhaps, prevented him from seeing the practical implications of various patterns of childrearing and family interaction. It fell to female analysts to attend more closely to the earlier weeks, months and years of life as well as to the nature of women's psychic and emotional development. It was these women, his daughter Anna as well as Karen Horney, Helene Deutsch, Melanie Klein, Marion Milner, Hanna Segal and Enid Balint, whose work decisively shifted psychoanalysis more in the direction of interpersonal relations. It is ironic, but perhaps not surprising, that it is the analysts Michael Balint, Ronald Fairbairn and Donald Winnicott who are remembered and credited with establishing 'object relations' rather than the female analysts who played such a large part, though Janet Sayers' (1991) *Mothering Psychoanalysis* does much to redress this as does Eric Rayner's (1991) *The Independent Mind in British Psychoanalysis*.

The Emergence of the 'Object Relations' School

In recent years, a number of books and papers have been published which show how the fuzzy and inevitably distorted memories of early experiences, which were often very frightening, survive and stay with us to affect and unconsciously shape the way we react to people and situations at work and home all through our lives (Segal, 1985). It is these fuzzy and idiosyncratic memories, or traces of memories, that are known as 'phantasies'. What is important about them is that they haunt us in peculiar ways and intervene in situations or relationships which have only the remotest, if any, connection with the original, usually painful, event.

To give a personal example: like most adults I do not like to think of myself as a jealous or envious person and probably rather overdo ensuring that I do not appear so. So I have often been surprised at how unsettled I can be by a particular sort of person, usually a colleague, and how this triggers a basically envious resolution to pull myself together and work harder. I easily imagine slights and feel 'put down' by them. Over the years, though, as I have seen that the people who 'produce' such feelings in me tend to look rather similar (tall and slender where I am short and square) and are upper-middle class, I have been forced to consider how this might be rooted in my reaction to the death of my twin sister at the age of sixteen months and my mother's very understandable grief for her. In this case a cultural and aesthetic polarization offers simply one more way to express highly charged and possibly unresolved feelings which started with infantile envy, became clouded by her death, got caught up with my mother's changed relation to me and the whole panoply of guilt and defences to deal with it, splitting, self-hate, and so on. All of these are expressed much later in the way that I try to define and think about myself; though, of course, such self-definitions are never wholly successful or secure.

The 'object relations' school (or, as it is sometimes called, the 'British' school) is largely associated with the work of Donald Winnicott. As an emerging 'school' or group it grew out of a dissatisfaction with the biologism of classical Freudian theory and a sense that the id/ego/superego scheme was too mechanistic and fragmenting. Though not without its own critics such as Andrew Samuels (1993) who claims that it is too individualistic, too committed to a developmental notion of causality and oblivious to the operation of group processes, the defining feature of the school was a commitment to seeing all affect and psychological growth as produced within a relationship – that is, within a social context.

Relationships were prior to any experience of the self and it was the experience of relationship with the mother's breast that was the basic 'stuff' of human life. The types of relationship between the subject (baby) and the object (mother usually) formed the raw material of the 'self'. It was establishment of this self that was the primary task of the baby and of the 'object relations' theorists who studied the process. Later relationships were viewed as shaped through anticipations based on the memory of that first experience, another word for which is fantasy or phantasy. The vocabulary used by the school can often seem obscure and confusing, especially as the term 'object' is used to mean a person, a part of a person, or a form of relationship that has been internalized. When the languages of education and psychoanalysis are brought together the potential for confusion is even greater, as 'subject' especially has several meanings. However, in this context, I use 'subject' in the sense of an academic discipline or body of knowledge and 'object' in the psychoanalytical sense, both as the goal to which instinctual energy is directed and as the other *person* in a relationship.

Winnicott's essential insight was to see that the teddy bears, blankets and other objects that babies get very attached to perform a crucial role in their emotional and cognitive growth and are the prototypes of all later intellectual tools. He called them, somewhat confusingly, 'transitional objects' or 'transitional phenomena'. At the start of life a confusion between felt wants and these being met, sometimes well and sometimes badly, was the lot of all babies. No environment was perfect or constant and all babies had moments of pain and frustration. It is the failure of needs being met that creates the basis for individuation. A baby whose needs were met virtually before they had a chance to feel them would never learn about self and other. As no such baby exists, Winnicott concentrated on the variety of ways babies dealt with the hit-and-miss mix of experiences that is their life at this stage. His whole view of psychological development centred on what happened between the mother and the baby and on the fluid, indeterminate area or space between them. He made these relations of reciprocity and this 'space' the theoretical centre of his work, for this was where he thought growth happened. As his ideas developed it became clear that the intermediate area did not have to be a space, it could be a thing, but whatever form it took he called it a 'transitional' object or 'transitional phenomenon'.

Fairly early on infants learn to deal with the inevitable frustrations of life (i.e., their mother not feeding, changing or cuddling them quickly enough, or simply by not being there instantly when wanted) by endowing something else, for example a toy or a blanket, with the capacity to bring about comfort. These substitutes had a number of special properties. They stood for something that was not the baby and yet they were wholly under the control of the baby. Neither 'self' nor 'other', these phenomena existed in the space between the two people and helped organize the emerging self as well as being the stuff of its creation. Their paradoxical or ambiguous nature was, according to Winnicott, absolutely essential. One of the greatest services a mother could do for her baby was to preserve the illusion that the baby had created what, in fact, it had only been offered, whether this was the breast or some other desired item. For the baby to grow it had to believe that it could be powerful, an agent; yet at some point it also needed to know about the real world in which its imaginings did not produce what was wanted. This confusion or illusion was very precious, and an essential stage in normal growth. It went on being important and, according to Winnicott, formed the basis of the human capacity for culture, which would be impossible without the capacity to imagine or to fantasize.

An integrated self (the aim of psychological growth) was, at best, a precarious achievement and, for some people, it could take a lifetime to secure. Winnicott stressed that before experiences are 'owned' they are 'shared' – shared, that is, with the mother, or primary caretaker, and essentially *confused* with her. Being tied up with the mother is *the primary experience*. The developmental task for the baby was to disentangle, detach and recognize senses and feelings as its own and not someone else's. Winnicott observed that one of the ways that babies achieve this gradual detachment and sense of self is by imbuing certain objects with personal and therefore *symbolic* value. These toys or blankets were fairly firmly under the control of the baby and provided it with the illusion/experience of enough power for an effective sense of self. As life and mothers were bound to be frustrating and inadequate, a solution to the ordinary experience of relative deprivation had to be found. Babies do this by finding comfort in blankets, teddies etc., which are neither self nor mother but something in between and which, most importantly, they can control. Incidentally, they also acquire the capacity for symbol formation and lay down the ground for all later growth and learning.

In the context of different emphases within psychoanalysis Winnicott allowed much more scope for 'the environment' to affect the course of development than did Melanie Klein, on whose work he initially depended. He saw emotional growth as not purely a matter of inner conflicts and their resolution, but of how the infant adapted to the environment and how that environment adapted to the infant. He is famous for having declared that there was no such thing as a baby, only a nursing couple, a mother and a child, and for showing how the baby had to grow out of the mother psychologically, just as it did physiologically. From this perspective 'transitional objects' help an infant to integrate their feelings and establish a sense of self as separate from another person. Only after this is achieved are they able to have a real relationship with another person (that is, one in which the otherness of the other is understood).

Humans learn to meet their own needs as best they can, and one of the ways they do this is by substitution. In the early months of life fingers can substitute for the breast and later blankets and cuddly toys also serve as comforters. The child has started its creative life. Later still, the meanings that were once idiosyncratic and personal become shared in a more mature sense. As Winnicott writes, culture (music, paintings etc.) is an inherited tradition, a pool of common humanity, to which individuals and groups of people may contribute and which they can draw from 'if [they] have somewhere to put what [they] find'. An infant is helped along the path of growth towards being able to function adequately as a human being by a series of illusions which conveniently obscure the difference between subjective and objective experiences and which the mother, or other caretaker, is usually good enough not to puncture.

In a sense psychoanalysis became the science of 'mothering' and it is this that provides one of the strongest grounds for turning to it to help explain school-based processes of gender formation. It is the predominance of women in teaching, especially in the early years, and the fact that teachers are emotionally 'in loco parentis' that makes it theoretically appropriate and it is through the quasi-parental relationship that gender enters schools, though putting it this way makes it seem as if gender is some additional 'extra' that we can choose to have or refuse. Obviously this is impossible, for we exist only within our genders; right from the start we cannot be genderless, though gender itself is not fixed. Indeed very little is ever fixed, though some arrangements are common enough for patterns to emerge, and the general predominance of women in childrearing is one of these. The acquisition of social and gender identities starts in this context. With female teachers and other staff mediating the child's experience of school, fantasies based on early familial experience are easily elicited and repeated.

It is this stress on the mother as environment that lends Winnicott's version of psychoanalysis and object relations to sociology and education, for each discipline also stresses the social construction of relationships and identity. Furthermore, a transitional object is something that gets lost and found again, repeatedly, and this makes the link with formal education and learning even more evident. For finding and losing is the experience of most learning, and particularly with complex and abstract material. Learning anything but the most basic skills does not fit the behaviourist model of incremental positive and negative reinforcement. If we read a difficult article ten times over we do not necessarily understand a little more at each reading, and understanding, if it comes at all, tends to come suddenly as a breakthrough (Jordan, 1968). Even then, after several readings comprehension can slip away for it is not secure, but easily lost and in need of being found again.

Although Winnicott's formulations of early psychic life made an impact, in part, because they departed from the prevailing psychoanalytic ideas of the time, and especially from Melanie Klein (Phillips, 1988), treating academic subjects as transitional objects, as I do in chapter 7, points up the continuities rather than the differences between Klein and Winnicott. The fact that some subjects, mathematics perhaps most publicly, are feared and others enjoyed much more seems to parallel the 'good' and the 'bad' breast that Klein suggests is part of all early life, or rather of infantile experience. For Klein, pain and pleasure, discrete good or bad experiences, precede any experience of the mother as a whole person. According to Klein it was a major achievement to realize that good and bad experiences might have the same source(s) and that although this recognition could occasionally be achieved, it was frequently lost again as our lives proceeded. By analogy there are bits of the environment that make you feel good about yourself and bits that do not and some of these bits, I shall argue, are school subjects.

Conclusion

This chapter has attempted to show that as feminism became more hospitable to psychoanalysis, and gender a more central topic in education, a convergence around the interpersonal was almost inevitable. If this area was to be theorized (and there were some external reasons why this was thought to be urgent) psychoanalysis had some attractions. Risks, however, are taken whenever psychoanalytical categories are used by those not trained as therapists, that is, when they are detached from clinical contexts or when they are applied to texts rather than to people. In addition, in almost any field, as writers move away from applied contexts they seem to make theoretical differences both more significant and more obstructive, indeed they often turn into obstacles to be vaulted over before researchers can get back to the problem that first interested them. Psychoanalysis is no exception and has the added problem that it attracts a sort of reverence which, when used in an interdisciplinary way, has the air of a traveller's tale whose awesome reports can be neither challenged nor verified. In turn, this has provoked the wrath of some philosophers who regard psychoanalytical ideas as untestable, and therefore as invalid.

Practising psychoanalysts wince at 'psychobabble' and non-psychoanalysts often view the appropriation of psychoanalytic ideas as a sort of adventurism or opportunism, or even as a grand, collective folly (Gellner, 1985; Somerville, 1989). Nevertheless, the object relations approach is supremely interpersonal and had been convincingly used to explain the gendered patterns of parenting. On the face of it, given that there are more than superficial similarities between teaching and parenting, it seems worth making a theoretical comparison. The question of 'Why do mothers mother?' can be asked of women teachers. Why do so many of them teach – especially when the labour market has become considerably less segregated than it once was? The answer, as I hope the next two chapters will show, lies in the forms of anxiety to which teachers and parents are prone and in the way that the organization of the school locks in with those anxieties.

Chapter 3

Anxiety and Defence Mechanisms: Driving Forces

Education is an anxiety-ridden enterprise as any child, parent, teacher or student knows. We worry about starting or choosing a school, changing school, leaving school, taking examinations, facing a class of pupils, having to teach a subject we do not know well enough or, at almost any age, talking to the head. Fears about whether teachers will be too strict, whether there will be too much homework and too many bullies, whether we will make friends, blight the transition to secondary school for almost all children and are exceedingly familiar. What is possibly more surprising is that education is also an anxiety-*driven* enterprise. Famously, the Education Act of 1870, which established a universal system of education for the working classes, is widely 'explained' as a response to the Franchise Act of 1867 and to the fears of the landed aristocracy that they would be overthrown. 'We must educate our masters' is one of the most quoted remarks of the nineteenth century and expresses the fear of what might happen once the labouring classes were enfranchised. The establishment of education for the poor was thus as much a measure to assuage a bourgeoisie frightened of revolution as it was a benefit for the poor themselves. Today it is fears about the superior academic performance of German or Japanese children, especially in science and mathematics, that has levered a rather static education system into change. So it is perhaps not surprising that collective, or sectional, anxieties lie at the heart of many educational arrangements.

In practical terms, formal education is anxiety-driven because, as organizations, schools and colleges are based on selection and a notion of cognitive and social development that might or might not be achieved. A model of 'normal' development is set up and, although the distribution of ability is expected to be 'normal', if a child fails to be spot-on or above the average a considerable amount of parental and teacher anxiety usually follows. This is almost unavoidable in a system that is arranged as a graded series of tests, examinations and selection procedures in which ultimate achievement is what counts rather than the degree of progress made from a range of starting points. In this system failure becomes more likely at each successive point and is, therefore, accompanied by more fear and anxiety.

Anxiety is produced not only in and by schools, but around them. The timing of the school day and juggling of meeting times with work causes worry and anxiety for many parents and, as state education is progressively underfunded, many more dither over the option of private schooling, the political implications of such a choice and whether they will be able to afford the fees. Whatever decision is made, worry about schooling starts even before a child arrives with its parents' concern to make the right choice. They continue with doubts or fears that the child will cry on being left, will not make friends or eat anything and might get hurt. Later, the mixed messages about attainment targets and rates of developmental progress, and the double-bind situation that arises from a denial of, or muddled accommodation to, sex-based developmental differences in primary-age schoolchildren take over as the pegs on which parental anxiety is hung. For the children, it is clear that there is much anxiety about the transition to secondary school and that this is tied up with, and followed by, the prospect of bullying and sexual harassment (Measor and Woods, 1984). They are expressed in, and amplified by, the frightening stories, or myths, that children tell each other of what will happen to them when they go to a new school, heads down the toilet and worse (Delamont, 1989, 1991). Anxieties are further and finally stoked by the sense that one's whole future might depend on what subjects are chosen at GCSE or 'A' level. And, for many, the later years of compulsory schooling are now dominated by worry about whether they will be succeeded by employment; whilst, for some parents, the time that their children are attempting Oxbridge entrance examinations and the worry about whether they will get a place is pure misery. Yet, after the first days at a new school, rather little is done to reduce anxiety or see it as a collective problem. Indeed, it is explicitly cultivated by schools when they want to impress on children how hard they must now work or how important the choices they are about to make are. It is used, and recommended, as an alternative to motivation, teachers being expected to adjust the 'right' level of anxiety to get the best effect on their pupils (Sutherland, 1983).

And, as fear and anxiety become more prominent, so do typical responses to them. For these reasons it is possible to argue that anxiety and coping with it is a central, structural, principle in much educational practice and that the effects of this are profound. Many of the specific features of schooling, for example, revision classes or mock examinations and the whole 'pastoral' system, are easily understood as ways of containing and limiting anxiety, but the approach can be extended to the organization of teaching and to the analysis of gender more broadly. Traditional gender roles and choice of stereotypic subjects and careers are 'playing safe' gender strategies and are much more likely to be encouraged under conditions of increased anxiety. This argument is not simply an individualistic one that applies to girls alone, though for some time the idea that girls or women might be more prone than boys to problems of anxiety, low self-esteem or fear of success was popular (Sassen, 1980; Horner, 1980). Rather it is that gender itself is a social defence mechanism. However, to make the case that the problem of gender and education is really one of anxiety and education it is useful to see how anxiety has been treated in social theory generally.

Social Life, Freud and Repression

The theme of anxiety as a typical reaction to social situations has been a long-running one in social thought. It is central to Georg Simmel's (1909) essay 'The Metropolis and Mental Life' and to Emil Durkheim's (1952) classic work on anomie as a cause of suicide. It runs through a whole raft of writers who have struggled to capture the American character and nearly always decide that it is predicated on anxiety. These include May (1950: *The Meaning of Anxiety*), the Lynds' (1929 and 1937 *Middletown* studies), Fromm (1942: *Fear of Freedom*), Riesman *et al.* (1950: *The Lonely Crowd*), McClelland (1953: *The Achievement Motive*) and Trilling (1961: *The Liberal Imagination*). This tradition has been continued by Christopher Lasch in a series of books, including *Haven in a Heartless World* (1977) and *The Culture of Narcissism* (1979), by Barbara Ehrenreich's *Fear of Falling: The Inner Life of the Middle Class* (1990) and by Rupert Wilkinson's (1984) account of toughness as the ideal and quintessential, though defensive, American attribute. Kai Erikson's (1966) *Wayward Puritans*, a study of the New England witch-hunts, offered a view of a community in which displaced anxiety and defensive projections were mobilized to keep a community founded on unity in the face of adversity going, whilst in Europe the German writer Ulrich Beck has dealt with similar issues in his book *Risk Society* (1992). The particular focus varies in all of these accounts, from a confusion over roles, lack of adequate fathering or cultural tradition, the intrinsic nature of cities, bureaucracies or organizations, through to guilt at affluence, fear of 'others' and risk generally. But in all of them there is an understanding that the source of anxiety is not uniquely individual but can stem from the social, economic political or technological conditions. In turn, these conditions offer individuals a chance to project their inner, psychic conflicts onto the larger, social issues which receive and embody those projections.

To a greater or lesser extent, all the above books and explanations are part of the Freudian heritage which placed anxiety and repression at the centre of social life. Crudely speaking, in Freudian terms, social life was a form of tension between individual pleasure-seeking drives or libido, and the knowledge that they could not be given into, but had to be repressed for the sake of society. This tension is a central plank of Freudian theory which also holds that one source of anxiety is brought on by a fear that repression might fail. In this way repressed libidinal energy and its consequence, anxiety, are placed at the very heart, not only of symptoms and neuroses, but of most social formations. From this perspective nearly all social phenomena are variations on the theme of repressed libidinal energy. Later analysts, such as Melanie Klein and Donald Winnicott, introduced a broader view of anxiety and tied it, not just to repression, but to the intense vulnerability of infancy; but they too made anxiety and various responses to it one of the major driving forces of human behaviour.

Overall, the influence of anxiety was profound. In the short run it encouraged the development of symptoms or neuroses (themselves forms of escape from anxiety which worked through the offer of immediate comfort) as well as a range of defence mechanisms. These mechanisms were quite normal in the sense that everyone uses them and they are rooted in the normal chaotic and contradictory experience of the first few weeks and months of life where the prime problem is to work out why and how the opposite and contradictory experiences of pleasure and frustration can have the same source (mother or 'breast'). Before the more mature understanding that objects and people are not constant and can be variable, unreliable and so on is grasped, a standard 'solution' is to treat the 'good' experience or person as different or separate from the 'bad' or frustrating one. This, in the psychoanalytical vocabulary, is called 'splitting' and, for a while, it works. It is simple and it preserves the good person, experience or memory as good and confines the bad to one place. In the psychic economy it also frees the child to hate the 'bad' object and vent their aggression or anger on it without any fear of damaging the 'good' one. Of course, sooner or later, these simplicities break down and the complexity or multiplicity of life and people has to be got to grips with. In Kleinian theory this is known as achieving 'the depressive position' which is, as its name implies, a painful learning stage but, because it involves a capacity to introject aspects of the good object, it enables the infant to grow and be marginally less vulnerable to the vagaries of life and the external world.

Out of this thumbnail sketch the important point is the account Freudians and Kleinians give of splitting and of projection and introjection as mechanisms for the transfer of experience and of making social connections. Traditionally, defences are viewed as limiting and dysfunctional, but they have another side which sociologists have picked up on, which is that defence mechanisms enable people to get on with their lives in some fashion. Social structures can do likewise and have the same contradictory quality: they enable and disable at the same time. The sociological studies listed earlier all build on Freud's view that social institutions are, to some extent, based on repressed libidinal energy and its defensive consequence, anxiety, though not always explicitly. However, the study that reveals the relationship between individual psychic need and social organization most clearly is Isabel Menzies Lyth's (1959) account of the nursing service of a general teaching hospital which highlights the conflict between what, in sociology, are sometimes called the 'manifest' and 'latent' functions of an organization. Well known in psychoanalytic fields, though not so in education or sociology, the themes of the paper can easily be transferred to other organizational settings such as schools. However, partly because it is so overtly functionalist (which in sociology is still a suspect approach) and partly because it is not well known outside the psychoanalytical or nursing studies community, it deserves to be described in some detail.

Isabel Menzies Lyth and the Nursing Study: Social Systems as a Defence Mechanism against Anxiety

The original task facing Menzies Lyth and her colleagues in the 1950s was to advise the hospital how it might stem the loss of trainee nurses and reduce staff/patient ratios. It was not to discuss how social systems could or should respond to the emotional needs and anxieties of their members, though the power of the paper was to show how one led to the other. Individual defence mechanisms such as splitting and projection had become commonplace as a way of describing individual behaviour, but to use the concept to describe an organization as having a similar strategy was a major breakthrough. The two sorts of defence mechanisms (social and individual) are not the same, though they may have linked and converging consequences. Individuals will make use of social arrangements for private psychic purposes and social systems may need to make arrangements along these lines for their members but, though the two processes may reinforce each other, they must be kept analytically separate.

In fact Menzies Lyth's starting point had been Elliot Jaques' (1955) work on how whole social systems could operate as a defence against persecutory anxiety emanating from several sources. Her contribution was to show how the intrinsically distressing nature of much nursing work could, all too easily, evoke feelings of anxiety which were in fact rooted in the nurses' own experience as babies. As she explains, 'The objective situation confronting the nurse bears a striking resemblance to the fantasy situations that exist in every individual in the deepest and most primitive levels of the mind'. For adult nurses this fantasy situation was very nearly matched in objective reality and they mapped, as we all do in varying degrees, the infantile fantasy situation onto the objective situation to produce a mixture of reality and fantasy.

However, if nurses were not to succumb to the strong feelings that arose from this combination of reality and fantasy they needed support and ways of dealing with the anxiety – which is where the organization could help. From the organizational perspective nurses had to be protected to some degree from their particular occupational hazards which included deep attachment to needy patients, grief and loss following those patients' death and contact with distraught relatives, and a general closeness to suffering. All of this could be overwhelming and disabling – hence the anxieties of individuals were an organizational problem which needed an organizational solution. However, although solutions were found and became the typical organizational structures, they had costs as well as benefits. Arrangements which worked at one level, containing and minimizing the otherwise disabling grief and anxiety, caused problems at another.

The traditions of nursing provided the protection needed, largely by splitting up the nurse-patient relationship and moving staff around so that no one nurse got totally involved with one or a few patients. An ideology was developed that denied the 'specialness' of any one patient and tasks were allocated so that one did all the bedpans, another all the meals. A 'good nurse' was not meant to mind being moved around or mind any particular task that she might be asked to do. Other elements of this institutionalized defence system included the excessive double checking of every task and referring of responsibility upwards. Though it worked well and meant that jobs got done, its rigidity created its own inefficiencies as well as making life unbearable for some nurses. It certainly helped nurses with some of the stress of nursing and the effects of feeling guilty: it meant that they could keep going and get on with the everyday tasks. But stereotypes of 'irresponsible junior nurses' abounded and responsibility was moved unidirectionally away from juniors towards seniors. All this served to minimize personal responsibility and the anxiety that went with it by mobilizing the primitive defences and splitting. But it was counter-productive too.

The system may have been fundamentally geared to meeting the unconscious need to reduce anxiety amongst the staff; but it also infantilized them, reduced the potential for 'job satisfaction' and peer support, and meant that many 'good nurses' gave up nursing altogether. Nurses were prevented from coping with the anxiety in more mature ways and were not given the chance to distinguish real anxiety, risk and danger from the distorted, primitive memories of the terrors of infancy. They were not allowed to grow through encountering and coping with it. Instead, they were encouraged to introject the hospital's defences and to lose their capacity for mature, creative thought and action and self-respect. In short, they were forced to regress.

The traditional nursing arrangements (hierarchical, fussy, ritualistic, rigid, depersonalizing and obscurantist) led to wastage and dissatisfaction amongst the nurses, especially the better ones, who were mature enough to need to exercise discretion and responsibility. However, the social arrangements fulfilled both social and psychological functions. In staffing terms there was actually a greater need for semi-skilled nurses than for fully trained ones, so the practice of using students on the wards fulfilled those requirements rather well.

It is possible to take from this account some broad generalizations about institutions which can be applied to schools and to the sexual divisions within them. Menzies Lyth's contribution to the sociology of organizations was to show that phenomena seen from one perspective as dysfunctional, for example nursing routines, could, from another, be highly functional. Even the 'wastage' that had seemed to be the hospital's problem was an essential and effective way of ensuring a good supply of semi-skilled workers. In a later paper (Menzies Lyth, 1989) she considers the general application of psychoanalytic insights to institutions through the medium of consultancy and lays out the grounds for seeing systems of establishing defences against anxiety as central to the functioning of many organizations. These rest, she argues, on the basic sociological units of roles, structures and work culture approached with psychoanalytic insight. The content of roles is, in fact, the product of projection: they are made up of the views of the self and others and the projection of others. When roles are combined to make hierarchical social structures they both allow and encourage further projection, both upwards and downwards. The more hierarchical the structure, the more likely it is that individuals will feel anxiety about whether they are up to the job and, similarly, the more likely they are to view both their superiors and inferiors within that structure (for example, matrons or nurses, teachers or pupils) in terms of their external position. That is, subordinates (nurses or pupils) will often project upwards onto a superior a belief in their own capacity, they will expect superiors or teachers to be competent (and attack them if they fail) but will concomitantly diminish their own sense of competence.

As Menzies Lyth notes, there is nothing magical about this process; it is conveyed through little interchanges like 'I will do that for you' which also carries the meaning of 'you cannot do it for yourself'. Drawing, in her later paper (1989), on the work of her colleague Alistair Bain, she describes how the content of roles is partially determined by projection systems which then contribute to the views held of the roles and those who occupy them by both those 'in' and 'out' of them. A step even nearer to sociology is taken up by Hinshelwood (1989) who details what he calls the 'projective life of institutions'. Social networks, he argues, are used by individuals to pass feeling states that they do not want to own along to others as a form of psychological defence by projection. The sum of all this 'affect' gives the network or institution its momentum and energy. As a consequence, the depleted individuals feel depersonalized and make remarks like 'this place is eating me up' because, psychologically, they have become fused with the group.

> [T]he individual becomes the raw material for the developing culture, its structure and activity. His unconscious investment in it is based on primitive mechanisms involving splitting. A split piece of experience comes adrift from one member and is projected as if it were a package, a discrete quantum of experience which, in the unconscious minds of individual members, can be taken in and given out. . . . A large institution feels inhuman because individuals literally lose themselves (or part of themselves) in it. Such an institution can also often force individuals to take in the projections of others. That person is then highly likely to feel imprisoned in a 'role' that is 'not them'. (Hinshelwood, 1989)

Hinshelwood goes on to argue that the depersonalizing effect on the individual of projective identification can produce what sociologists call alienation for the group, and alienation is the scourge of much education. It comes through as boredom, underachievement or delinquency, but its source is the dissipation of authentic feeling within affective networks and the exploitation of it within social networks. In the United States concern about this has arisen in discussions of jobs which exploit 'emotional labour' (Hochschild, 1983; Gergen, 1991) but it is a much broader feature of institutional life.

Schools and Schooling as Social Defence Mechanisms: Some Parallels

If we turn to schools and ask whether Menzies Lyth's analysis can be applied, there are several points of convergence. In the first place there is a belief in 'the child' or, rather, in the belief that all children are equal which bears comparison with the equality of 'the patient'. In both instances it leads to a denial of significant differences between children (or patients) at both a political and personal level. Although the 'all children are equal' claim is theoretically tied to some concept of educational equality and citizenship rights, and appears to be 'progressive' when it leads to schools refusing to come to terms with genuine differences based on gender, race, class and even ability, it can have the opposite effect – it can perpetuate inequality. It also enables the institution to avoid making difficult decisions about teaching practice and the 'fair' use of scarce resources. If everyone is equal there is no problem; whereas if the difficult allocative decisions are faced up to they may elicit painful memories and remind teachers of their own experiences as the 'favoured' or the 'not favoured' one, either at home or school. Hence the 'all children are equal' principle can function as a defence against either acknowledging current differences or remembering the feelings about old ones and how they were treated.

Another similarity that can be drawn is that between the nurses' increasing feeling of their own inadequacy and the common feeling among teachers that they cannot do anything else, that their skills are 'non-transferable' and that they are stuck in teaching (Buchan and Weyman, 1989). So deep is the feeling of 'stuckness' that before the recession truly began to bite an organization was set up to help teachers get out of teaching and was known by the acronym of the PIT. That there is either a large swathe of unhappy teachers who would rather be doing other jobs or a 'problem' of wastage is not surprising. The occupations of both nursing and teaching have historically relied upon limited labour market opportunities for women to deliver a steady supply of high-quality, well-educated candidates. The lack of other opportunities for clever girls meant that nursing and teaching were well supplied: they went into teaching and stayed there. Even now, when there is a greater sympathy towards equal opportunities but an even stronger concern about shortages, one can read labour force projections which refer to a need to 'draft' a quarter of all the suitably qualified *female* school leavers.

The costs to the individual of doing a job that they are not happy in, and that does not utilize their talents or reward them adequately, are obviously high for the individual concerned; but they are also high for the organizations that employ them. Given the appallingly skewed distribution of senior posts in education between men and women, especially in primary education where one in two men employed are either heads or deputies, there are bound to be many female teachers operating at levels well below their capacities which, as Eliott Jaques (1970) demonstrated, is as bad as working at a level that is above it. In boom times this means large turnover costs, but even if 'retention' is 'good', a polarized and divided or strongly hierarchical system encourages negative projections and damages all those within it. Those at the bottom lose confidence in themselves and 'give up', whilst those at the top are threatened by more competent juniors and become defensive as a result. Individuals and organizations suffer.

Yet many of the recent changes in education (as in the health service) are moving in the direction of social systems which increase hierarchy yet reduce the chances of the majority of nurses or teachers to achieve higher pay or more responsibility. Just as nursing grades have been redesignated, licensed teachers and pay systems which reduce scale points or impose controversial performance-related pay schemes have been introduced. As pay goes down teachers, and nurses, are less trusted and systems rather than individuals are relied upon to deliver quality and maintain standards: this is known in management terms as TQM or 'Total Quality Management'. The other side of this is a reduction in teachers' discretion and pay schemes which tend to concentrate on outputs rather than process, the facilitating of which remains the central task of teaching. In the name of raising standards, many of the 1989 reforms of increasing testing and imposing a national curriculum have had de-skilling effects – reducing the scope and need for teachers' intellectual discretion and turning them into the deliverers of packages and schemes. Whilst the rationale for this may be to mitigate the effects of the poorest teachers, it must also encourage the more lively and independent-minded teacher to leave teaching when economic circumstances permit; and if they do not leave teaching altogether they certainly leave the classroom (Hargreaves, 1994), especially if they are men. Those who stay (which includes a lot of good women teachers) have to adjust to loss of autonomy and frustration.

Teaching is a notoriously isolated and isolating work experience which leads teachers to have a poor perception of themselves and their abilities. They do not know what their colleagues actually do in the classroom and are prey to fears that, whatever it is, others do it better. Jennifer Nias' (1989) study of primary teachers stresses the privateness of teaching; only the pupils know how effectively or not they have taught and, as she puts it, 'teaching has a bottomless appetite for the investment of scarce personal resources'. It is no wonder that more want to leave than actually do (see James Kelman's autobiographical novel *A Disaffection* (1989) for an account of the cost of teaching and its capacity to engender anxiety in teachers as a result of their identification with pupils). In turn, this produces an occupational culture in which not only is good work hard to recognize and reward, but a series of myths about the 'good' or 'bad' teacher arise instead.

In his doctoral thesis on the teaching of reading John Gray (1976) attempted to identify the difference between 'good and bad' teachers and whether 'good teaching practice' made a significant difference to how well children learned. Gray found that, though heads were generally confident that they could 'tell' a good teacher and reputations as 'good' or 'bad' teachers flourished, he became increasingly sceptical of such claims to know and see good teaching performance. He could find no way of establishing empirically that 'good' teachers did anything substantially different from those who did not enjoy that reputation. Yet this research, plus the general conviction that there are good and bad teachers, suggests that the good and bad bits of individuals are projected into reputations which are themselves defences aimed at reducing anxiety. Though these reputations seem to displace anxiety for some they actually increase it for all. Those who are not favoured become jealous, those who are fear losing that reputation, and a degree of paranoia develops all round. A groundless and exaggerated ideal of perfection is erected, in front of which anyone able to be the slightest bit self-reflective is liable to feel inadequate.

For teachers left in the isolation of the classroom, anxieties simply multiply; they remain untested against the observation of other teachers and of other classes. In the end teachers fear inspection and appraisal because neither individually nor socially have there been realistic opportunities to overcome the fears or gain assurances that what they are doing is adequate. In Gray's research all the teachers, even those rated the 'best', were unrealistic. They overestimated the amount of time that they spent in what they defined as 'best practice' (in this case how often they heard pupils read), which suggests that they all had a need to 'think themselves up' and identify with an ideal self. Reputations, therefore, are based on extremely volatile and subjective factors. The more they are acted upon, or treated as 'real' (for example, by allocating discretionary pay), the more they will make organizations responsive to unconscious factors. Although the following is not the sort of interpretation offered by Gray of his data it may, nevertheless, confirm Hinshelwood's view of individuals as able to use social networks to pass on to others certain feeling states or elements of identity which they wish to disown. In this case a sort of psychological defence by projection is at work whereby the qualities and affects of individuals come to be possessed by the social network to form the energy for institutional activity. As a result, the individual's experiences and feelings are depersonalized and,

> the individual becomes the raw material for the developing culture
> ... his unconscious investment in it is based on primitive mecha-
> nisms involving splitting. A split piece of experience comes adrift
> from one member and is projected as if it were a 'package'.
> (Hinshelwood, 1989)

Individuals lose themselves, feel unloved and unvalued or 'alienated'. This process goes on within and between schools. Writ large, a very similar set of processes underlie the spontaneous social divisions which develop between girls and boys in mixed schools, and in the public stereotypes of girls' schools and boys' schools.

It is hard for teachers to see rewards in their work. What they have put into it easily gets 'lost'. If pupils or students pass examinations, it is the pupils' or students' success, not the teachers'. And, though attention has turned in recent years to stress as a significant feature of teaching (Cole and Walker, 1989), the popular image of teachers as having a fairly 'cushy' life with long holidays persists, and can be felt as an unfair attack. As a working environment a school actually has a number of disadvantages. It is noisy, there is little 'downtime', exposure to infections is high and there are few 'perks' or secondary gains. Unlike working situations which are predominantly with other adults of the same age there are relatively few opportunities for teachers to 'meet new people'. Teachers are not allowed to get familiar with students although, from the teachers' side, there is evidence that teachers actually feel happier about teaching when they are younger and more closely identified with their pupils (Petersen, 1984). As teachers age, they lose this affinity and need to develop other bases for teaching, or other defences.

As individuals, when we struggle to overcome gender or age stereotypes, we are struggling to come to terms with the projection of others. This goes on all the time. Mostly, sociologists have referred to this in terms of roles, or role making and role taking (Turner, 1962) but because, as suggested in the last chapter, this approach became unfashionable, the concept's essential dependence on psychoanalytic ideas remained unexplored. Menzies Lyth, on the other hand, suggested that

> the success and viability of a social institution [is] intimately connected with the techniques it uses to contain anxiety ... [and] understanding this aspect of the functioning of a social institution is an important diagnostic tool and therapeutic tool in facilitating social change ... the resistance to social change is likely to be greatest in institutions whose social defence systems are dominated by primitive psychic defence mechanisms, those which have been collectively described by Melanie Klein as paranoid-schizoid. (Menzies Lyth, 1989)

These, then, are the processes of splitting, denial of feelings, detachment, projection and collusion that are part and parcel of everyday school life. It does not require much effort to see the same general processes in the increasing extent and depth of gender divisions as children progress through school. Sex-stereotyped subject choices, single-sex friendship groups, sport, barracking, teasing and jeering, and the firm association of seniority with maleness are cultural and organizational features of the school. They conform, as did the work arrangements in the teaching hospital Menzies Lyth studied, to the psychic defences of splitting, of projecting and of denying responsibility. This can be seen at all levels of education, but it is most acute in secondary school where earlier and more primitive fears of falling to pieces/failure, of cruelty and revenge, of jealousy and envy are again aroused.

Schools as the Producers of Anxiety and Sex-Differentiated Responses to Anxiety

Secondary schools lend themselves to this sort of analysis because anxiety is built into their organizational structures, it is their 'social technology'. They could not function without reports, tests, examinations and selection, all of which both produce 'new' and channel 'old' anxiety. Selective entry (for some schools) and the prospect, as well as the reality, of examinations, combine to produce high levels of stress and anxiety which rise each year and, quite probably, will go through the roof when testing at all the four 'key stages' is fully established in addition to the existing crunch points of GCSE and 'A' levels.

Yet few people willingly repeat the experience of sitting examinations and the adrenalin 'junkie' who takes his or her pleasure in this form is almost as rare as the bungee jumper. For much of a child's time at school the high levels of anxiety produced by examinations play a crucial role in maintaining discipline. Schools cannot be run without them. Sometimes they aid or produce motivation, but more often they are a substitute for it. The long-term increase in pupils entering examinations is usually welcomed as a sign of rising standards, but it has to be understood as an organizational necessity. In the context of compulsory education, discipline is a perpetual problem and in Britain it became even more so for the non-examination pupils when the school leaving age was twice raised, from 14 to 15 and then from 15 to 16. At the time only a minority of pupils sat 'O' level examinations, the labour market was buoyant and pupils needed some rationale for remaining at school. The solution was a new, lower-level examination, the Certificate of Secondary Education (CSE), which was later combined with 'O' levels to make the current single examination system of General Certificate of Secondary Education (GCSE). Whatever view is taken about standards and the proliferation of examinations within secondary and further education, it is a form of social technology intimately related to the need to maintain social control. It is always claimed that motivation is increased when more of the school population takes examinations, though it might be more accurate to say that fear and anxiety do the job of motivation. Of course, if jobs are not forthcoming and too many attacks are made on 'A' levels as being easier to get, and therefore less worth having, this may be set to decline. Whatever the future holds, the recent past has shown that the experience of schooling has changed. The moments of anxiety have increased: they affect more pupils, and account for more of their time in education.

Another example of how anxieties may be produced collectively can be seen through the effects of recent British educational reforms. The enforced and rapid changes to schools, colleges and universities in Britain have disrupted good and bad practice alike, and the creation of league tables and published examination results are making the 'choice' of schools ever more critical. Ballots to determine whether schools should 'opt out' of local authority control and receive funding direct from the Department for Education to become 'grant-maintained' create a high level of local animosity, division and tension. In no way can they be said to enhance community life. All who have had experience of them say they were dreadful times. Several authorities have reported difficulties in recruiting heads, and discussions of stress in teaching are ubiquitous. However, this is not wholly a new problem, brought about solely by recent reforms: a generation of student teachers have grown up on a sociological literature that explicitly addresses teaching in terms of 'coping strategies' (Hargreaves, 1986; Woods, 1990), which is another way of getting at the educationally-induced anxieties.

As education gets more politicized, anxieties increase and so, I suggest, do gender divisions. Again, recent history illustrates this point. It is clearly significant that the schools choosing to become 'grant-maintained' are 'over represented' by single-sex schools. Before grant-maintained schools were introduced, 13 per cent of secondary schools were single sex; now, 30 per cent of grant-maintained schools are single-sex. It is hard to assess the true extent of parental or professional support for single-sex education, as it is easily compounded and confused with other desires, such as a wish to support a local school against closure, a desire for selective education, a desire to protect daughters from being harassed, a desire to keep them away from boys, or a conviction that single-sex schools provide a better learning environment.

However, as life gets harder, there is a tendency to retreat from innovation and prefer 'traditional' solutions. As the Act champions 'parent power' and the right to choose, we may expect to see more appeal cases from pupils denied entry to single-sex schools, as in the cases of Hertfordshire and Birmingham, as more parents want it for their children. In Hertfordshire a girl wanting to attend St Albans Girls' School used the grounds that the Local Education Authority had provided enough places for boys at a single-sex school, but not for girls who wanted single-sex education. Much the same situation was faced by Birmingham after the opting-out of some single-sex schools had left it with an unequal number of single-sex places for each sex. Many more LEAs could find themselves similarly caught out. With falling rolls and an over-supply of secondary school places, LEAs were bound to look at single-sex schools as prime candidates for closure, unless they had a firm and prior commitment to these schools on social and educational grounds. Whether they had such a commitment depended on a peculiar mix of local politics and personal prejudice. In this context parents have become a 'wild card'. Whether for reasons of ethnic integrity, fear of the disruption of school closure or conviction that single-sex schooling is best, parents have begun to fight to save single-sex schools, via the courts or through the provisions for opting out. As the Act aims to increase parent power and tip the balance in their favour, it increases the chances of local ballots and local conflict.

Gender, Fear and Anxiety

If schooling is anxiety-driven, so too are gender divisions, and what we may be witnessing in schools and universities is the convergence of two systems with a similar momentum behind them. A clear example of fear driving gender relations can be seen in the rituals and arrangements surrounding menstruation and childbirth (Redgrove and Shuttle, 1978). In many societies both are seen as polluting and fear-laden. Witch-hunts, female circumcision and purdah may also be demonstrations of how fears are mobilized to maintain deeply divided and unequal relations between the sexes. In attempting to understand these institutions it is often argued that there is an aggressive projection onto women, through abuse, of men's own fears of weakness. The weaker women become socially, the more contact with them has the potential to tar men by association: contact therefore has to be controlled or limited to reproduction. Thus run arguments about why men tend to be more violent towards women than women are to men. These rest on the idea that the deeper the social difference, the more is invested psychologically in maintaining it (Smith, 1989) and although such arguments do not claim that fear produces the deep divisions, once they are there, fear reproduces them.

There are now ample descriptions of how gender divisions appear quite early in children's school careers, many of which can be described as responses to anxiety. Socialization into a masculine, not to say macho, culture in primary schools prevents boys from forming, or remaining, friends with girls, even if they would like to. Raphaela Best (1983) calls this the 'third curriculum' in which small boys have to make the grade in terms of toughness, just as they do in the other two curricula (the formal and the informal). Friendship with the opposite sex is 'fraternizing', and it is fear of ridicule, of being seen as weak, of taunts that there might be a romantic attachment, that keep the sexes apart. At a slightly older age it is girls who have to walk an ever more perilous tightrope, constrained by the fear that as they mature sexually they will attract comments about their appearance which are barely distinguishable from abusive names and, once such labels have been applied, they fear being unable to shake them off (Lesko, 1988). The choice for girls, as depicted by Sue Lees (1986, 1993), is that of being seen as a 'drag' or a 'slag'. Much of the aggressive talk, sexual innuendo and put-downs delivered by boys to girls (Walker, 1988; Jones and Mahony, 1989), and sometimes returned, can be seen as signs of the boys' anxiety about their own sexual development (Tosh and Roper, 1991; Cohen, 1990). It is even possible that the 'tolerance' schools often appear to have of this phenomenon is complicit. Subcultures, or gangs, are often largely single-sex and, as such, are a sort of solution to some of the specific anxieties of schooling.

No one at school cares for you like your parents and the frantic search for a friend is, in part, an attempt to get some order into the chaos that large schools represent when you first enter them. The situation is reminiscent of a baby's first experience of the world as unbearably chaotic. In infancy the job of the person taking care of the baby is to hold the baby together, psychologically as well as physically, in order to provide some containment or sense of coherence. In the school, when a similar situation is met again, either a 'best friend' or a little group can perform the same function. The common observation that bullies are dealing with their own pain at not being loved is easy to fit into this general model of anxiety, as Jane Ellwood and Margaret Oke's (1987) description of their analytic work with a small group of difficult boys in a single-sex boys' school suggests. The boys in their group were part of a subculture that centred on hopelessness, and being 'hard'. Both were required within the group and meant that feelings were disowned; so there was a constant search for a scapegoat to carry the disowned pain. The subculture, or group to which they belonged, operated as 'a defence against feelings of dependency' and the boys' cynicism protected them from the risk of disappointment (if they chanced admitting to the possibility that the school might have something good to offer them). Ultimately, rather pessimistic about the whole exercise, Ellwood and Oke nevertheless demonstrate that by attempting analytic group work with the boys they challenged their defences; in the process the boys struggled to establish control while the two women offered containment.

In one sense the linking of anxiety with gender differences in educational performance is not new. Margaret Sutherland (1983), for example, comments and expands on the view that women and girls are generically more anxious than men and boys, and that it is this which leads them to 'underachieve', to fail to think of themselves as capable, or to apply for senior positions, to limit their aspirations and even to 'fear' success. Accepting that girls generally are more anxious than boys and that a little anxiety can be a good thing, the tenor of her argument is to consider how teachers can adjust the dose. However, she views anxiety very much as a problem for individual girls and of classroom management, as do most of the psychologists on whose work she draws, for example, Ralph Turner (1964). Throughout the period from the late 1960s to the 1980s, a psychological paradigm prevailed which suggested that girls feared success, perhaps failure too, had low self-esteem, played safe, avoided risk and learned 'helplessness' (Horner, 1974; Sassen, 1980). Kay Deaux's

(1977) work in particular rested on a grasp of the powerful impact of anxiety. Interested in how boys and girls understood their varying levels of academic performance she showed that when girls did better than expected, they tended to explain their success in terms of unpredictable factors such as luck whereas, if they did less well academically than they expected, they were inclined to explain this outcome as evidence of their low ability. Boys, on the other hand, tended to do the opposite. They invoked bad luck when they did poorly and innate ability when they did well. This attribution research has profound implications for how gender divisions might increase and deepen under conditions of intense anxiety. In anticipation of future anxiety (and girls' reactions to it) it is clear that girls are often counselled to take the intermediate rather than advanced mathematics exams. There have also been suggestions that women fail to get as many first class degrees as their work deserves because they cannot take the pressure of finals and are more scared of examinations than men (Judd, 1991; McCrum, 1994).

In the mid-1980s, Australian educational administrators were sufficiently impressed by suggestions that the problem of gender and education was that girls had low self-esteem to introduce a range of intervention programmes aimed at raising it and, it was hoped, their educational performance. However, Renshaw (1990) argues that this approach was fundamentally misguided. In the first place, the evidence that girls had low self-esteem was poor, though there was evidence of boys having a greater confidence; in the second, it rested on the fallacy that traits can be isolated from their context. Lastly, but most culpably, it displaced attention from the school practices and 'blamed the victim'. It left open the question of whether low or high self-esteem followed or preceded achievement and treated 'self-esteem' as a gender-neutral attribute, which it is not. As Renshaw points out, blowing your own trumpet is inconsistent with femininity, whereas 'learned helplessness' is not. A more fruitful approach might have been to rethink the curriculum and to attend to structural features such as the double standards which led boys to be criticized for matters of presentation (the good presentation of girls and the poor presentation of boys being taken for granted) and girls to be criticized for matters of content. But institutions find it difficult to criticize themselves rather than individuals within them. With children especially, who are socially weak, it is they who are subject to attempts to change whilst the settings in which they live and which 'construct' them are left alone or have only token alterations made.

The whole episode, apart from illustrating the difficulty of defining and measuring the term self-esteem, or of launching into intervention programmes on the basis of inadequate research, suggests two further points.

First, though it may not always be possible to measure emotional states directly, either individually or collectively, their effects may still be felt. Second, one of the more obvious ways of seeing the effects (and therefore existence) of collective anxieties is through norms, stereotypes, ideologies, representations, repressions and denials. The prevalence and persistence of stereotypes is closely tied up with individual and collective anxiety, for all stereotyping is fundamentally defensive (Billig, 1989). It offers a reason *not* to get close, *not* to allow detailed information to disrupt perceptions and force deeper thought, which can be confusing and delay action.

By simplifying and being economical with intellectual energy, stereotyping reduces anxiety. A lecture that is too detailed, too hedged about with qualifications, is generally less successful than one which makes a bold sweep of an argument, and much education in both the formal and 'hidden' curriculum is like this. Education is rather distinguished by the credence given to non-expert opinion, by the idea that everyone has a view and a right to voice it. Whilst good and democratic in one sense, public opinion has also been much manipulated through the concept of 'parental choice' (Brown, 1990) and is a force largely governed by emotions and not facts. In practice it is based on defensive stereotypes rather than on information, and when a topic of public concern touches on gender there is an even stronger tendency to ignore or avoid data and cling to deeply held convictions. An example of this is the widespread belief that coeducation must really be better than single-sex education. It is hard to dent this belief or direct attention to what actually happens in coeducational schools rather than what the speaker hopes should happen. As the penultimate chapter shows, the whole debate is a case study in anxiety-driven stereotypes. And very similar to the argument about coeducation is the one about educational standards. Fears that standards are falling are periodically voiced and form the justification for political campaigns such as the 1993 Conservative 'Back to Basics'. However, over the same period in which standards are meant to have fallen, measures such as numbers of pupils entering and passing examinations have consistently risen. Nevertheless, 'falling educational standards' is an excellent campaign tactic, it arouses short-term anxiety, is generally perceived as someone else's problem and leaves intact a broader and unquestioned assumption of progress.

Macro Trends

There are no easily available sources of data on trends in fear and anxiety although they may be inferred from rising sales of home protection devices and car phones, the rise of 'lady cabs' and the dramatic decline in the number of children getting themselves to and from school on their own. Even as recently as 1971, 80 per cent of children took themselves off to school, but by 1993 this had fallen to 9 per cent (Hillman, 1993). The favoured explanation for this is a rise in parental fears that their children might be abducted or run over. This is not to say that there is no real foundation to such fears, but that living with fear has become a major determinant of behaviour. We carry a capacity for anxiety with us all the time which, though it derives primarily from our personal circumstances and biography, can be added to by our experience of the world around us and by particular institutions. Economists often talk of 'morale' and of what might be happening to 'consumer confidence', especially in the later stages of an economic recession when attention is keenly focused on whether people will begin to risk buying goods or taking out mortgages, which is another example of how broad economic conditions resonate with, and tap into, a personal capacity for anxiety. For anxiety, like all emotions, is essentially transferable and labile. When economic or political scenarios are gloomy they produce collective emotional reactions, even from those not immediately affected by redundancy and unemployment.

Changes in everyday life, including living with a sense of risk and fear as expressed, for example, by women not wanting to walk alone at night for fear of rape and mugging, may be part of a global process. Somewhat along these lines Ulrich Beck (1992) has argued that living with high levels of risk, both real and perceived, is the price we pay for modernity. Air crashes, Chernobyl-type pollution disasters, global warming and so on are phenomena which affect us all but which are outside our control, or even most governments' control. Yet we continue to take them into account at an everyday level if we can. In making his case about risk as a general phenomenon Beck makes much of the contradictory position of women within modern societies, namely that whilst they live within the modern world they are still subject to a form of feudalism in terms of personal relationships. It is gender relations that have failed to modernize. Whatever scenarios are projected for the future this approach makes it abundantly clear that there is a close connection between trends on fear, risk and anxiety and gender.

Chapter 4

Parenting and Teaching: Being Emotionally 'In Loco Parentis'

The unconscious slips which lead pupils to call their mothers 'Miss' or their teachers 'Mum' show clearly that teachers occupy an emotional space left by their parents. The issue is what happens in that space and why being emotionally 'in loco parentis' is important for understanding how schools contribute to the social construction of gender. From an object relations perspective mistakes will be made in all directions, pupils may confuse teachers with parents and vice versa, teachers may confuse pupils with their own children, if they have them, or with themselves as children and other teachers with memories of their own parents or teachers because all relationships are to some degree conditioned by earlier ones. But in teaching this slippage has more resonance or significance because the parallels are more overt and at root, if the quality of the teaching depends on the quality of the relationship, these mutual confusions lie at the heart of the teaching process.

The Patriarchal Principle of Schooling

In the educational context the idea of being 'in loco parentis' is shorthand for describing the obligations teachers have to care for children as a good, or at least average, parent would. It is the bottom line for judging teacher performance. Yet exactly what being a good-enough parent means is rarely spelt out, except when there is a crisis and a child is damaged. At that point a standard of 'average parental care' is used to judge negligence and assess how much a school, teacher or local authority's insurance company can be made to pay. Beyond being a code for assessing where responsibility for injury or accident lies the term is not very helpful and may seem irrelevant today as we no longer live in a feudal society where service to a lord and apprenticeship are central features, or in one where parenting can be summarily and legally reduced to the right to punish and/or profit from a child's labour. Economic necessity and primogeniture no longer consign most young people, peasants or aristocrats, to periods of residence in somebody else's house where they would probably be ill-treated and where the law was needed to ensure some form of damage limitation.

But modern systems of education still draw on the principle of being in loco parentis as an adjunct to compulsory education, the potential for damage is still present and teachers are still expected to view their responsibilities as quasi-parental. Thus the concept is not wholly anachronistic and can be extended beyond a legal or moral interpretation to include feelings. It is because teachers are 'in loco parentis' that they can influence children at all and it is because of this odd relationship that schools become major players in the way that gender is formed and reformed. If gender is a social construction, it is based on past as well as present relationships, and the relationships that pupils bring to school and mesh in with their teachers and their teachers' prior experience are relationships formed at home with parents and siblings. Gender is not abstract, it is personal and embedded in particular experiences. The focus of this chapter is, therefore, on the muddling and muddying of the roles of parent and teacher and the anxieties which arise from that confusion, and with the unconscious and reciprocal processes of identification which occur between pupils and teachers. For it is in this ground that the school-based seeds of gender identities are sown. The expectation that teachers regard themselves as being 'in loco parentis', when many, especially at the start of their careers, have had no experience of parenting their own children, invites teachers to attach themselves against something that is, and only can be, a fantasy.

Teaching has only relatively recently become a 'caring' profession. It used to be much more disciplinarian and militaristic. Drill, rote learning, discipline and tests defined it long before 'child-centredness' became the prevailing pedagogy. Though teaching is obviously grafted onto some notion of parenting, the 'parent' was not originally the mother, but the father; and it is quite clear from the legal judgments which use the concept that being 'in loco parentis' concerned what fathers could do to their children, that is, punish them, enjoy the fruits of their labour and marry them off (Shaw, 1977). Historically, mothering was not appealed to or even recognized. The 'good' teacher was derived from the harsh, but 'good', father.

Today, the ground rules have changed and the effective parent of educational discourse has subtly shifted from being the father to whoever is the most 'emotionally involved'. Although this is not legally spelt out, this is now usually the mother, as illustrated by the procedures made for schools to 'opt out' from local authority control and become grant-maintained. Schools have to ballot parents before they can opt out, but who counts as a 'parent' has been extended to include step-parents or other adults who live with and, in a practical way, are committed to the child. This means that the right to decide on the fate of the school is now tied to personal investment in the child and not solely to kinship rights. Though a small example, it shows how far the state has moved from viewing the rights of parents as a matter of discipline and economic benefit to one of emotional investment. Where once the cane was proudly wielded, use of it is now regarded as excessive and a cause for anxiety about the emotional state of the beater. Indeed, in 1993 a British man won an award for damages as a result of being beaten some years earlier at his private school, Brighton College.

These shifts are paralleled by and related to what is often described as the feminization of teaching. This is usually taken just to mean that the gender composition of the profession has changed, and that there are more women teachers. But it should also include changes to the idea of the 'good teacher' which, because of feminization in the first sense, has got closer to the idea of the 'good parent' and, by implication, to the 'good mother'. Nurturing, in particular, has taken over from discipline at home and at school or, at least, has become just as important. As a consequence of both sorts of feminization, the sorts of relationships that are now possible between pupils and teachers and between schools and parents have altered at both formal and unconscious levels. A rigid separation of home and school is no longer thought a prerequisite for successful teaching, rather the opposite: a 'good', cooperative relationship is viewed as desirable, even necessary. The gap, or boundary, between home and school has been reduced rather than stressed and this, both socially and psychologically, invites parents, teachers and pupils to merge. At the same time the criteria for judging teachers have, in general, got closer to being based on what mothers do. In terms of the general argument, the scope for anxiety about teaching has been substantially increased since the profession became more feminized. Though the ideal of the good teacher has got closer to the ideal of the good mother, it is no easier to achieve for much the same reasons – namely that at the unconscious level part of being a good mother means letting oneself be 'used up'. Whilst the model of teaching based on fathering may have been temporarily ousted by one based on mothering, this shift has not improved women teachers' career prospects in either emotional or practical terms.

More women enter the teaching profession (a feature normally associated with progress) but the bases of gender division within teaching remain as entrenched, as 'familial' and as defensive as ever. Indeed, the higher number of women entering the profession can unconsciously reinforce the couple motif in appointments at all levels, and make the rise of the men even more assured through the 'glass escalator' effect whereby women form the troops for men to lead. A concern to maintain a 'balance' of masculinity and femininity can often block the careers of women if 'too many' women are perceived as 'getting on'. When combined with the 'crowding' that leads women to compete primarily with each other for the same jobs, these two features can actually diminish the chances of success in teaching for an individual. Whilst men rarely suffer from being 'overrepresented', women frequently do. Bizarrely, perhaps, the culmination of this process are the recent British educational reforms which have redefined the jobs of senior teachers as managers, administrators and accountants, thereby reintroducing 'maleness' into the definition of teaching, and enhancing the careers and prospects of male teachers.

This is simply a new phase of the general, patriarchal principle which underpins schooling (Spender, 1981; Blackmore, 1993). It can be seen most clearly in the pattern of appointments to headships. The idea of the head as a sort of father dies hard, as does the sense that it is tricky to appoint a woman over a man and, since most state schools became mixed, the chances of women getting headships has actually decreased. It is still common for women, however competent, professional or expert, to get no further than deputy, not least because of the unwritten rule of the 'parental couple' (Richardson, 1973) where the implicit message is that schools are best run by a parental couple, a mother and a father, but that the ultimate authority lies with the father. In an earlier era this was embodied in the post of 'senior mistress' which was as far as a woman in a mixed school could expect to get. Formal and informal arrangements such as these clearly boost the sense of men's authority by incorporating gender into the formal hierarchy, and are an example of what Michael Marland (1983b) calls 'staffing for sexism'. Though they are perhaps not promoted quite as explicitly as they once were, they are extraordinarily persistent and visible in the prevailing pattern of appointments. Governing bodies and appointing committees frequently express a preference, not always unconscious, for maintaining patriarchal authority, and are self-conscious when the formula is departed from. But times change, and although it is possible to read off from the political changes a reinforcement of patriarchy as a model for teaching, the emotional preconditions for teaching are changing as families and social relations change.

Parenting and the Emotional Infrastructure of Teaching

Parenting remains the template for teaching at an unconscious level, and the process of teaching still works through a series of unconscious identifications. Like a number of other occupations, such as social work and counselling, feelings related to parenting (how one does it and how one was parented) form the emotional infrastructure of the job. Again, as with other similar 'people-work' jobs, working with children invites the teacher, at some level, to match their inner preoccupations with some aspect of the broader social world. In the case of teaching it is with the memory and the ideal of parenting. Yet parenting (real or symbolic) has not attracted a lot of attention, either as a subject in its own right or as the basis of a series of occupations which have been grafted onto it.

There are studies of why people might choose or refuse parenthood (Dowrick and Grundberg, 1980), or why the bulk of parenting falls to women (Chodorow, 1978; Trebilcott, 1984), but there is little about the emotional side of being 'in loco parentis' and indeed, very little about what it feels like to be a parent, even from the psychoanalytic literature where it might be expected. As Alan Shuttleworth (1985), who is an exception to the rule, observes, this is surprising, for 'being a parent or the love of children is as profound and central a feeling as any in adult life'. He adds that where parenthood is discussed it tends to be in terms of the crisis of birth and the beginning of parenthood and not very often in terms of the later 'long haul' stages which are probably more typical than the dramatic beginnings. Most relationships start off with great expectations and move through various stages of disillusionment. This is as true of parents and their new babies as of lovers of each other or of primary school teachers as compared to secondary school teachers. Euphoria soon gives way to depletion and worry about how good or bad a job one is doing and, either in relation to actual children or work that symbolizes the desire to be creative, there is an inbuilt and ever-present threat of depression and despair. This depression and its accompanying anxiety, or 'burn-out', is the occupational hazard of teaching and is, as Willard Waller (1932) described it, exactly 'what teaching does to teachers'. First-hand accounts of it can be found in almost any of the now numerous life histories of teachers.

If depression is an occupational hazard of teaching, one way of coping is through the psychological defence of 'splitting', and the form that this takes for many teachers is through a stereotyping given meaning by the school. Just as parents regard teachers as coming in two sorts, 'good' and 'duff', teachers view pupils and parents as 'good' and 'bad' too. The culture of the school helps maintain the belief, and indeed the hope, that there are 'good' teachers; but it also makes it hard to recognize them in practice. 'Good teachers' are really fantasies, just as 'good mothers' are: they exist in reputation, not reality, and are the products of projection. Being the good or perfect teacher is very close to wanting to be, or to supplant, a perfect mother. And, because most of us are neither perfect teachers not perfect mothers, we have to grapple with our fears of failure. And fail we will, because a degree of failure is guaranteed by the social structures in which the practice of teaching takes place. The ideals largely exist so that we can persecute ourselves, and in many settings the idealizations retain their power precisely because there are so few opportunities to process them or to distinguish fantasy from reality.

The isolation of teaching, especially, leaves the teacher alone with their own anxieties and fantasies and relatively ignorant of how other teachers teach. How teachers deal with this situation varies according to their gender and to the models of the good teacher that they aspire to, which are not the same for men and women. As teaching has become a more female-dominated profession, the implicit and explicit models of teaching underpinning it have changed. There has not been a simple shift from an ideal based on fathering towards one based on mothering; rather a conflict between the two has grown. And, as the two models of parenting/teaching become institutionally grounded, it is harder for either to dominate, hence a pattern in educational thought of swings, 'progressive' to 'traditional' and back again. Consciously, of course, there is a uni-sex ideal of professionalism that makes no concession to feminization. But anxieties about performance flourish in the gap between the conscious and the unconscious ideals and, in crisis conditions, encourage defensive reactions which in educational contexts tend to take the form of reverting to more traditional gender relations.

Teachers' Anxieties

Many of the work anxieties peculiar to the teaching profession such as not being skilled at anything else, of being 'stuck', of being 'second-rate' or being 'only' a semi-profession, of being undervalued, of not being 'good enough', or of losing control, have their psychological and social roots in the place of teaching both as a profession of the upwardly mobile and one which women can enter with relative ease. But some of the anxieties are also rooted in a systematic confusion of the roles of parent and teacher and in the confusion between teaching as mothering and teaching as fathering. There is a strong resemblance, in the stereotypical fears of teachers, to the fears and feelings of motherhood in general. In a certain sense, mothering is a 'non-transferable' skill; it is not valorized in the market place and, though women do a lot of caring for other children, one can only really mother one's own children. The widely held view that teachers do not know anything about the 'outside world' is a sign, not just of the low esteem in which teaching is held, but also that the school or college represents a 'parent' and that those who work in them have yet to 'grow up' and 'leave home'. Yet, in the sense of being responsible for a lot of children, teachers have to be ultra-adult and, unconsciously, teaching remains firmly grafted onto the parental role. This means that many of the specific anxieties teachers have to grapple with stem from that quasi-parental role.

Moreover, the gap between reality and fantasy is widening. As practical conditions worsen for real parents (Hewitt and Leach, 1994; Etzioni, 1994), ideals, or rather fantasies, of 'intact' two-parent families are bandied around with little regard for how they might be realized. Much the same is happening in teaching. Real teachers are 'burned out' in high rates of stress while being exhorted to improve their performance, just as lone parents are. In both cases, teachers and parents and individuals can feel persecuted by impossibly high ideals, so it is important to understand where these ideals come from. Some of them are political constructions, but some of them are not. The rooting out of 'bad teachers' is part of the justification for appraisal, performance-related pay, etc., but it also depends on a contrast with the myth of the 'good teacher'. A *Guardian* leader (25 July 1994) argued that educational reform, though long overdue and promised by all political parties, was more or less impossible to deliver because there were still so many 'bad' teachers still in the system who could not be rooted out even in twenty years. This sort of commentary contributes to the polarized and defensive stereotypes of 'good' and 'bad' teachers. It makes teachers feel uncomfortable and insecure. Life becomes a knife edge. One is either good or bad, not simply 'good enough'; and which side of the line one falls can be a matter of chance. Members of other occupations such as those in the army or the police do not fear in the same way that they will never get another job, and though many in fact have difficulties, this tends to come as a shock.

Teachers undoubtedly feel, and are, overworked and persecuted. Much of the excess load has come about as a consequence of the national curriculum and the newly imposed demand for regular testing. But some of it has an internal source. It was significant that the British teacher unions did not get round to formally objecting to increased workloads when the impact was being borne by primary school teachers who were mainly women, and only took legal action when the impact was felt in the secondary schools where there are more men. One interpretation of this is cynical. Men's interests count for more than women's. Another is that women are subject to 'superwoman' ideals, they try to take on all that is thrown at them, for doing so satisfies a particular and gendered fantasy of omnipotence.

Teacher Power and Fantasies of Omnipotence

Nowadays most teachers do not believe that gender is 'natural' or fixed, or that men are better able to occupy positions of power. The few who do are exceptions and often rather apologetic about it. It is far more common to encounter teachers worried about their relative inability to arrest the process of gender division and differentiation that goes on around them, in spite of efforts to prevent it. Teachers, nevertheless, get blamed if they attempt to widen consciousness of gender and sexuality, or if they do not. When a head of a London primary school explained her rejection of an offer of cheap seats to *Romeo and Juliet* on the grounds that it promoted only heterosexual love she was threatened with suspension, despite overwhelming support from parents and official commendations of her excellence as a head. When it hit the headlines this case seemed quite unreasonable, though it drew on the widely held belief that teachers 'model' gender and are therefore responsible for reproducing it. Being gendered themselves they cannot help this, but the criticisms imply that schools and teachers are meant to do the impossible.

And doing the impossible, or being expected to, is where the fantasies about teachers originate. Look at the noticeboard in almost any school office (or doctor's surgery) for comic postcards about demands for the impossible to be done yesterday and for examples of defensive reactions to such demands. The demands come out of a fundamental, unrealistic and essentially fantasy-based sense of the power of teachers (or doctors). The omnipotence that is projected onto them is the first and most important sign that teachers are related to on the basis of infantile fantasies about parents. As with parents, their real influence is generally far less than that which is publicly attributed to them.

It would be silly to deny that teachers ever influence children, but they do so in ways that both they and the children are largely unaware of. The impact of a widely cited study, *Pygmalion in the Classroom* (Rosenthal and Jacobson, 1983), in educational discourse is especially interesting. Perhaps one of the best known of all educational research projects, it was based on a trick whereby teachers were fed false information about the IQ scores of a small number of pupils, picked at random. In this experiment teachers were set up to expect better performances from a number of pupils, who were said to be underachieving on the basis of their measured intelligence. In due course the children did much better than they had previously and the point of the study, which was to demonstrate that teachers' expectations could be experimentally isolated and manipulated and show that such expectations could affect academic achievement, was made. Its popularity is both an acknowledgment of how much teachers' influence pupils is unconscious and a sign of how hungry readers are for evidence that teachers are truly all-powerful. Yet, though normally discussed in the context of 'teacher effects', the study can be read as being about teachers' vulnerability. The yearning for evidence of teachers' power was not in order to celebrate that power, but to strengthen the basis for blaming teachers. Though, I believe, it has never been successfully replicated, it is widely cited because it resonates with widely shared fantasies about teachers and their omnipotence.

The Perfect Teacher or the Perfect Mother?

In this sense, there is a striking similarity between the way that teachers are viewed and responded to by both pupils and adults, and the ways that mothers are viewed. In an influential paper, 'The Fantasy of the Perfect Mother', Nancy Chodorow and Susan Contratto (1982) argue that feminist writing on motherhood had, despite itself, failed to escape from the culturally induced myth of idealized mothering. Their list of the feminists writing in the 1970s who had displayed despair at the impossibility of mothering is impressive: it includes Alice Rossi, Nancy Friday, Dorothy Dinnerstein, Judith Arcana, Adrienne Rich, Kate Millett and Jane Flax. All contributed to a contradictory account of mothers as being too powerful and, at the same time, of the job of mothering being too difficult. Mothers destroyed their daughters and their sons, and being a mother destroyed women. It denied them individuality, sexuality and company; or it pitched them into a world dominated by unspeakable fantasies of death and aggression. According to Chodorow and Contratto the root of the problem for these writers was their failure to understand childhood or to revise prevailing theories of child development. Though the feminists they cite appear to criticize the cultural ideal of the perfect mother by pointing to the social conditions which prevent its realization, they nevertheless support and continue the other side of mother-idealization, which is mother-hating.

Drawing from and reflecting a cultural ideology and infantile sense of infantile need and maternal responsibility for the outcomes of child rearing, feminists begin by identifying with the child and blaming the mother, or by expecting her to be more than perfect. Cultural ideology and fantasy can also lead to idealisation of maternal life from the point of view of the mother, as in the writing of Rossi and Rich. More often, the belief in total infantile need and maternal responsibility, and identification with the angry child, lead to a maternal identification that is in turn full of rage and fear, and a sense that the conditions of patriarchy totally oppress mothers and isolate them with their child. (Chodorow and Contratto, 1982, p. 67)

They stress that if the perfect mother is a fantasy, then so too are the child's needs and that

Feminist views of mothering, as mother and as daughter, have united infantile fantasies and a culturally child-centred perspective with a myth of maternal omnipotence, creating a totalistic, extreme, yet fragmented view of mothering and the mother-child relation in which both mother and child are paradoxically victim yet omnipotent. (Chodorow and Contratto, 1982, p. 71)

It takes little to transpose this perspective to teaching. The 'perfect teacher' has a lot in common with the 'perfect mother' as it, too, rests as much on a failure to fully understand parenting as on the 'feminization' of the teaching profession, important though this is. For if being a mother is hard, so is teaching, especially if the intellectual discipline of pedagogy is either absent or of such low status that it could only be explained in terms of a general dislike of children (Simon, 1985). Even where there was an idea of pedagogy that took mothering into account it did so, according to Carolyn Steedman (1985), in a thoroughly ideological way. Working-class mothers were either romanticized as intuitive earth mothers who trainee teachers should emulate, or they were utterly incompetent and in need of re-education by virtually any middle-class woman. Steedman views the ideological and class-based component of teacher training as an almost insuperable obstacle to the identification of teachers with the mothers of their working-class pupils, and thus to their effective teaching. In terms of how psychological identification works this is somewhat questionable, though a standard of middle-class normality by which working-class children were unfavourably judged may indeed have clouded the teachers' conscious judgments.

While the fantasy of the 'perfect teacher' may not exert as strong a grip on all teachers as the fantasy of the 'perfect mother' does on most mothers, to the extent that it does, it operates in the same way. It is widely felt as an appropriate goal to aim for, and has become ever more so since the teaching profession was feminized. The male notion of the good teacher is less personal than the female one though, of course, many male teachers are proud of good relations with their classes. Male teachers still quit the classroom and take on administrative and managerial jobs more than female teachers for reasons that are not wholly to do with money and promotion (Strober and Tyack, 1980; Shakeshaft, 1987). They are promoted for different reasons to women (a source of annoyance to the unpromoted women) and their managerial potential is sought and valued more than their classroom skills. Male teachers are not expected to draw on parental 'instincts' to guide them in their practice, whereas most female teachers are, whether or not they are mothers. Being a poor classroom teacher or lecturer is rarely an obstacle to men's promotion. In higher education this is quite explicit: teaching is not highly rated or taken into account in making decisions on academic rewards.

Women who choose teaching, especially primary school teaching, usually think of themselves as liking children, rather than teaching a subject, and they are attracted by the sense of 'wholeness' of the community of the primary school. Certainly, the teachers in Jennifer Nias' (1989) study stressed how important it was to them to 'feel at one with the class'. Repeatedly they singled this out as their best experience of teaching, which demonstrates that it was indeed a merged, undifferentiated ideal that they strove for. As Nias notes, it is unlikely that many of the teachers she interviewed had read Martin Buber, but they all spoke as if they had. Marilyn Joyce's (1987) account of what it meant to be a feminist primary school teacher similarly illustrates a general commitment to a 'whole philosophy' approach and suggests that what may be distinctive about women's orientation to teaching is indeed a relational and holistic approach, a broad moral stance that, according to Carol Gilligan (1982), is typical of women. Indeed, this may well account for why women teachers predominantly prefer working in junior and infant schools rather than in secondary schools.

All these accounts seem to confirm Chodorow's view that it is in seeking to remain in the merged unindividuated state that women are led to mothering and to substitute mothering, that is, to teaching. Teaching offers an opportunity to match inner preoccupations with some aspect of the wider world, as a number of autobiographical accounts suggest. Both Sophie Freud Lowenstein (1980) and Madeleine Grumet (1988) describe how teaching rescued them in mid-life from flailing and failing social identities. Grumet celebrates the opportunity to mother that teaching provides and incorporates it in her revised version of pedagogy. In Lowenstein's case, finding a 'passion' for teaching enabled her to avoid depression and overcome the narcissism which she saw as its cause. Channelling her energies into teaching helped integrate earlier emotional investments from her desire to be the best behaved child in Vienna (she was Sigmund Freud's granddaughter!) to being a good mother, wife and social worker and, later, a good teacher. Teaching, she claimed, made her feel autonomous and powerful and, for this, she celebrated it.

However, her description of her career can be read in another way. The moment she decided to enter teaching came with the chance to offer a course on the parent-teacher relationship for teachers in training: an area about which, as she says, she had plenty of personal experience. Teaching, although Lowenstein does not quite say it, was both her escape from mothering and the place where, when she applied the commitment of mothering, she got it right and got public acclaim. Reading between the lines, it seems that the time and energy she poured into her work were unconsciously aimed at getting a degree of praise and affirmation that may well have been unrealistic and fantasy-based. Though clearly writing her account as a middle-aged woman, Lowenstein shows every sign of being dominated by the fantasy of the 'perfect girl' which Lynne Brown and Carol Gilligan (1992) argue is the start of the undoing of most adolescent girls. It is the doomed attempt to conform to the 'perfect girl' fantasy that makes young girls lose touch with much of the knowledge that they initially possess about themselves, about others and about relationships; but which they progressively deny because, especially as it involves conflict, it does not fit in with the persona of the 'perfect girl'. Lowenstein calls teaching her passion and recognizes that passions, by definition, are addictive and enslaving, but she claims that this one did not make her dependent on other people. Yet this honest and open self-portrait is also a little schizoid. It portrays someone keen to be thought of as a good friend, but who also guards her time jealously, someone who is not a loner, but capable of solitude. The strong impression is of someone still striving to be *das bravste Kind von Wien*. The account of the teaching phase can be read as another phase of overinvestment, just like the overinvestment in her first child that she so regretted and saw work as an exit from. Perhaps not feeling sufficiently appreciated as a child she later had to demonstrate superwoman-type powers to compensate. The piece is a brave and honest one, and it seems to me to represent the feelings of many women teachers.

Ideals of Parents and Pupils

The sense that one can do better than the other is held to by both teachers and parents. Teachers believe that they could parent the children better than the natural parents and many parents believe that they could do just as good, or better, a job than the teachers. And if teachers have unrealistic ideals or fantasies for themselves, they also have exemplary ideals or fantasies about ideal pupils and ideal parents which, in varying degrees, may be shared by those parents and pupils. For most teachers the good parent is one who cooperates with the organizational goals of the school, gets the children to school on time with a good breakfast inside them, does not demand frequent meetings with teachers and unstintingly works for the school fundraising events. This parent can come into school at times convenient to the school and is usually, implicitly, a mother (though her gender is hidden under the generic term 'parent'). Parents, for their part, project much of their worries about their children onto the teachers. The good teacher is what the ideal parent would like to be, she or he never gets cross with the child, keeps control all the time, produces learning and doesn't have to struggle to do it. This good teacher leaves the parent free to storm into the school in anger if the teachers gets cross, raises their voice or hits a child. Teachers have 'to get it right' within a year, and if they do not, then they tend to blame the parent.

Schools clearly vary according to how easily the school/home or parent/teacher boundary is breached. In some schools relations are very fraught, PTAs are banned, parents' evening are kept to the minimum, and teachers often live as far from the school as possible. Even in generally successful schools teachers will complain that it is difficult both to get some parents into school and to keep others out – the boundary being both terribly important and hard to get right. Much of the boundary-related problems are about fear and anxiety. Some parents find that all contact with schools revives in them childhood memories, and their unwillingness to venture foot over the door is based on a reluctance to feel inadequate and juvenile again. The head of a very successful primary school once told me how an open-ended question to parents of the sort 'What do you like/not like about the school?' had revealed considerable anxiety about not knowing what was going on in the curriculum. Yet the same head noted how difficult it was to reduce this anxiety, and that whilst parents would come into school in reasonable numbers for a meeting called 'Help Your Child at Maths' – which seemed to be about *their* child – a meeting covering the same material but titled a 'Maths Curriculum Evening' would produce a poor turnout.

If we turn from the ideals of parents and teachers to ideals of pupils there is one feature which stands out and it is that, in addition to being hard-working, well-behaved and successful, the ideal pupil is probably male. There are many hard-working, well-behaved and successful girls, who are much appreciated by their teachers, but there are grounds for thinking that in schools, and in educational discourse more broadly, there is a fantasy of the 'ideal' pupil as male and that this affects how teaching is conducted. At the most simple level this may help account for the frequently observed gender differences in amount of teacher-pupil interaction, with boys getting more interaction than girls, of both a positive and negative kind.

In a description of teaching by Nel Noddings (1984) the teacher being addressed is clearly female whilst the child is clearly male. Noddings urges the teachers to 'receive and accept the student's feeling towards the subject matter' and instructs how she should

> look at it and listen though his eyes and ears. How else can she interpret the subject matter for him? As she exercises this inclusion, she accepts *his* motives, reaches towards what *he* intends ... the special gift of the teacher, then, is to receive the student, to look for the subject with him. Her commitment is to him, the cared-for, and he is – through that commitment – set free to pursue his legitimate projects.

The emphases are in the original and Noddings seems unabashed by the implicit sexism, but she is not alone in this stance. In nearly all the work that has attempted to get to grips with the emotional meanings of teaching there is often a celebration of the fulfilment either through vicarious mothering or escape from it.

There are several signs that catering for boys has, both consciously and unconsciously, dominated educational provision. For most of this century the rhetoric of educational reform has been in terms of increasing the opportunities for the working-class boy. In Scotland it is the 'lad o' pairts' (Gray, McPherson and Raffe, 1983), not the 'lassie', who is mythologized. A good part of the surprise, and even despair, when sociologists began to show how firmly the middle classes had retained their grip on the expanded educational opportunities which followed in stages after the Second World War, came from a failure to anticipate that it would be girls from the middle class, rather than boys from the working class, who took up the extra places, especially in higher education. At the informal level, boys receive more interaction with teachers (Spender, 1980) and, in the days of the eleven-plus examination, scores for the pass rate were adjusted to accommodate boys' generally poorer performance than girls' at the same age (Goldstein, 1986).

Even the dyslexia lobby may be seen as an organization for boys. Although estimates vary, the ratio of boys to girls suffering from dyslexia range from 3:1 and 10:1. Thus any organization which campaigns for more awareness of dyslexia is effectively campaigning for a better deal for boys. In a similar way, public support for coeducation may also be inadvertently based on a sense of boys' needs taking precedence over girls'. Though it is hard to demonstrate conclusively, not only do boys' problems with schools cause more general worry, boys' poorer school performance is felt to be more threatening by teachers, especially women teachers. All the above examples suggest that anxiety about boys' education has been greater than public (and private) anxiety about girls' education. The legacy of this, in a culture which now explicitly supports gender equality in education, has gone underground, but it persists in the unconscious and implicit masculinity of the 'ideal pupil' and in the teachers' responses to the anxieties that teaching brings out in them. The conclusion, therefore, is that the way teachers deal with their anxieties has gendered consequences for pupils.

In a situation predicated on fantasy it should not be surprising that the fantasy of the perfect teacher is both the cause of many teacher anxieties and a defensive coping mechanism. If a way of 'coping' with an impossible situation, say a class of screaming or unwilling children, is to resort to some form of fantasy of omnipotence, then the ideal of the perfect teacher who can meet the differing needs of a whole class may be one such defensive fantasy, produced simultaneously by the teacher, to persecute themselves for failing to meet the ideal, and by the culture which denies the reality of teaching. At the national level the lurch into testing, auditing and league tables, though driven primarily by ideology, is also a defensive, punitive response to the strains of teachers working in the shadow of an impossible ideal. Most people who enter teaching have left the profession for good after five or six years and although this is clearly affected by the large number of women taking a break to have a family, even for them it is often a face-saving way of dealing with the strain of teaching.

Men and Women Teachers' Responses to Anxiety

The form of anxiety that teachers are often most open about is discipline and keeping control. These problems preoccupy student teachers and a good many others, even those with years of experience. As a rule of thumb, keeping control is widely taken as a sign of a good teacher. Rather oddly, control of a class is viewed as something that a teacher cannot have too much of. Most teachers will argue that being authoritarian and having control are not the same, and there are few who think it possible to be a good teacher without control. Control of a class is far from easy, and on it hangs a teacher's reputation. Even more than knowledge, control is the basic tool of the trade, mercurial and easily lost, even by teachers of many years' experience. For women, without the advantages of height, a deep voice and greater social authority, this problem is especially acute. Though many male teachers fail to control their classes, and many female teachers are proud that they can, the majority of women teachers undoubtedly start off feeling disadvantaged. Vivian Gussin Paley (1984) writes about how female kindergarten teachers, knowing that a male head (himself escaped from classroom teaching) may be roaming the corridors, alter their teaching practice. Becoming pre-occupied with keeping down the noise levels out of a fear that noise will be interpreted as loss of control she may, quite unintentionally, repress even further the small boys in her class whose play demands more noise. For the responsive and sensitive teacher this may go right against their belief in what good teaching should be like.

The organizational consultant Sheila Ernst (1989) suggests that whilst both sexes resort to the strategies of splitting and regression, each does it in a way that excludes the other. The masculine mode typically elevates masculine qualities such as risk-taking, mastery, setting and meeting targets, and offers 'satisfaction' through the production of tangible outcomes. By contrast, the feminine mode stresses nurturance, listening, facilitating. The projected fantasy that 'satisfies' the female teacher or administrator is an unconscious subscription to the power of love and infinite maternal capacity to make things right. In this mode teaching is directly equated with love, with sexual relations and with the idea of infants/pupils needing to use up their mothers/teachers so that teachers under the influence of this fantasy will, masochistically, take on too much and willingly sacrifice themselves. The outcome of each of these fantasies, produced in the front of the classroom and in other educational settings, may well explain the question posed by Strober and Tyack (1980) of 'Why do women teach and men manage?' The answer is that each is driven by a gender-specific fantasy as much as because competing strands in educational thought have pitched teaching as fathering against teaching as mothering.

When female teachers insist that they have 'children eating out of their hands' and can keep control without resorting to violence or shouting, or that 'their personalities are enough', they are sometimes defensively claiming a personal charisma and engaging in a form of sexual competition. Let me make it clear, I do not believe that men are better at teaching or at controlling classes, but that each sex is driven by different fears and fantasies and each is undermined in different ways. For both sexes, beneath the vocabulary of classroom control are the twin fears and fantasies about omnipotence and chaos. Power is experienced by both as something magical which is easily lost, and much of their behaviour is guided by that fear of loss and descent into chaos. However, the other side of the fear about loss of control is the fantasy of omnipotence and it is this that teachers have to work at. What is so painful about teaching is that these twins, fear of loss of control and the fantasy of omnipotence, are ever present, though they tend to be dealt with somewhat differently by men and women.

Teaching is a very draining, enervating activity. We often use an imagery of being 'drained' or 'eaten up' which expresses just how much of oneself has to be 'given' in the teaching relationship. Sandra Acker's (1995) description of teachers in a Bristol primary school repeatedly homes in on their exhaustion, self-exploitation and inability to set boundaries around their work – as well as on the failure of others (often spouses) to recognize how hard the work is. As some teachers get locked into this form of occupation (usually women), their continuation in teaching needs explanation: it is not simply a matter of there being few alternatives. Of course, there are many external and sexist reasons why men get promoted out of the classroom more than women, but there are also internal ones. There is a masochistic element to women's teaching. Carolyn Steedman (1987) called schools 'prison-houses', not just because there were few other jobs available, but because the teachers within them were caught in a contradiction. They could not teach their charges effectively because, in the absence of any proper pedagogy, teaching was meant to be an extension of mothering and, as middle-class women, they simply could not be *like* the mothers of their pupils. Whether or not class differences really prevent identification on all levels is a moot point, but the responsibilites women hold seem often inherently contradictory and it may be this that keeps women in teaching. Frigga Haug (1992) has argued that responsibility for women is largely the product of a disordered society, and that a sense of individual responsibility comes about when general rules break down. She writes: 'Women are positioned at the meeting point of individual lives and the exorbitant claims of society, and acquiesce without flinching. They would rather be torn apart than give up or enlarge this unreasonable responsibility'.

Women's characteristic masochism simply describes their efforts to accept this situation. As Haug writes, responsibility manifests itself as an irksome compensation for the faults of others.... Love is one of the crucial factors in this structure, and with it there is the circumstance that in our market-dominated society a large proportion of women are unable to reproduce themselves in terms of the dominant currency. Where everything is exchanged for money, they earn none, or at least less than they need to live. This makes their situation as incalculable and as unconfined as love itself. They feel that they always give too little, and sense that they are neither loved nor themselves sufficiently loving to enable them to perform the Herculean tasks of maintaining the social order. (Haug, 1992)

Teaching is often equated with love, and women take responsibility towards their pupils more personally than men. This squares with the more general finding of a gender difference in relation to ethical behaviour. Carol Gilligan (1982) argues that women make the issues of relationship and the personal consequences for individuals central to their way of resolving moral dilemmas, whereas men more often appeal to abstract principle for a solution. Men get just as drained by teaching as women but they will not tolerate it for so long, they are not so locked into self-punishing routines and do not subscribe to the 'perfect girl' syndrome. To use a personal example, I once dreamt that I was actually being crucified and that the very nails which were being driven into me were shaped as homunculi students. There are, of course, many ways of interpreting this dream but I have no doubt that both consciously and unconsciously I aspired to be a perfect teacher (Christ?), despaired at ever achieving this aim and, in my dream, could only relate to the pain of teaching as my death.

Teachers, of course, were once children and they carry into their teaching as adults some of their own difficulties about learning. Indeed, many enter teaching because they are locked into unresolved conflicts and anxieties. However, these have personal, not social origins, and need to be distinguished as such. It is the social origins of teachers' anxieties that are important and these lie, increasingly, in the feminization of teaching. Most teachers, but female teachers especially, are subject to unrealistic expectations of nurturance, patience, empathy and knowledge. Like mothers, they tend to be related to first, through idealization and later through rage and denigration. This shift from idealization to denigration can be taken further by considering the parallels and connections between feeding and learning and gender.

Learning as Feeding

If children relate to teachers in ways that are similar to, and derived from, their experience of their parents (and to one parent in particular) it is very likely that, at an unconscious level, the process of learning will be linked to feeding and being fed. Just as mothers and teachers get confused so, at an unconscious level, can feeding and learning. Success or failure in learning may, therefore, depend on the actual and internalized experiences of feeding that a child brings to school. As Julia Segal (1985) puts it,

> It seems . . . that our ability to learn is related to phantasies of taking in good food and good people who love us as babies and small children. Difficulties in learning, just as difficulties with our digestion or eating habits or with friendships, may all be closely connected with the phantasies we developed as infants around the processes of taking in, and to do with what we felt when we took in.

Ischa Salzberger-Wittenberg (1983) and her colleagues use the feeding metaphor freely to explain learning difficulties as resulting from a conflict between envy and dependency. Though they do not specifically address the issue of gender, all their examples imply it. For example, in a chapter on denigratory relationships, Gianna Henry describes two boys who had both learning and feeding difficulties and comments that as learning and feeding are both about ingestion, a combination of intolerance of dependency and envy might make it very difficult for a boy to accept that the person offering food or teaching had anything good to offer or, indeed, to take it in if they did. When she describes idealization, another defensive strategy, her examples are of girls. This accords with the widely held belief that girls are more prone than boys to developing 'crushes' and to what Janice Raymond (1986) calls their 'passion for friendship'. Of course, not all boys denigrate their mothers and not all girls have crushes, but denigration and idealization are both strategies to avoid facing up to the complexity of experience. If the denigration of others is tied to a defensive idealization of the self, then a defensive idealization of others is also closely tied to low self-esteem or denigration of the self. In a society where women are socially devalued it may be harder for some boys at some stages to learn from women at all, just as it is hard for women to believe in their abilities. It is certainly very common in higher education for students, of both sexes, to be disappointed when they find that their lecturers are female, and this may not just be a matter of status and presumed ability. Denigration of others is related to a defensive idealization of the self. If one is feeling weak and vulnerable it is a common solution to project that onto someone else. For boys, the separation argument would suggest, this is a permanent possibility. If separation from the mother or mother figure is only achieved at some cost, that cost includes denigrating what was denied. For girls, subject to the same general social values, denigrating the self and idealizing others is simply culturally congruent.

But there is an element of struggle that may be as important as the feeding experience itself. The form that the struggles take to feed and be fed, to resist and reject, either learning or food, are clearly power struggles and from fairly early on the form that these struggles take in the classroom are differentiated by sex which may, in turn, stem from sex-related patterns of idealization or denigration. We know that in practice mothers concern themselves more over their children's progress at school than do fathers (David, 1993), but it is possible that the anxiety and agitation created around school performance creates distinctly different crises for mothers in relation to their sons and their daughters. It seems important that the people most involved in feeding are women, and the greater involvement of women in teaching and in feeding has implications for an interplay between the public realms of educational provision and the psychic role that it affects.

The way that new food is presented and the stage at which it is presented can be crucial. As the mother of two children who are extremely reluctant to try new foods I cannot help but wonder whether by breastfeeding for a relatively long time I made my children miss a stage when they would have accepted and enjoyed new foods more eagerly or, perhaps, I was so desperate to wean them at eighteen months that I created such fear and tension in the process that they hung on to what was being denied them. When, on the rare occasions they now do try new foods, they alternate each mouthful with huge gulps of milk. I will probably never know whether I breastfed for too long or mishandled weaning, but certainly switching from milk to any other food is a real and continuing struggle. Meal times are characterized by much movement from the table and general avoidance behaviour. Now that they are older and do their homework on the kitchen table the same pattern exists: lots of distraction and fiddling with anything to hand, trips to get drinks to both ease and escape from the task in hand.

Many teachers and/or parents are quite explicit about their attempts to make food/learning palatable and often use a meal-based notion of a 'balanced curriculum' compared to a 'balanced diet'. Pairs of associations are set against each other so that just as protein is meant to balance carbohydrate, so more and less valuable subjects or masculine and feminine ones are expected to be mixed. To use another food-based metaphor, the mixture is a way of sugaring the pill. If any of this is plausible it is also likely that the task of reading and writing, which dominate the early years of education and are very gendered in their typical patterns of development, may bear the traces of unconscious conflicts over feeding. Teachers, books and classrooms may all trigger buried, and not so buried, memories. The equation of feeding with learning is more than a metaphor, it is a mode of relating and is a further example of the 'object relations' approach. However, the main point of linking teaching to feeding and the feeding metaphor is, first, to show how deeply inscribed it is into much educational theory and practice and, second, to trace gender differences in learning patterns to gender differences in feeding or, rather, in identification with those who do most of the feeding – mothers.

Feeding is not the only way in which an imagery based on parenting infuses the theory and practice of teaching. We talk quite easily and openly of a 'parent discipline', but there are many other examples. These include the swings of fashion for and against 'traditional' or 'child-centred' methods of teaching and the split and oscillation between skills-based and knowledge-based models of learning. Rosemary Clarke (1988) describes much contemporary education as a sort of force feeding where information is gobbled up at someone else's suggestion, without regard to whether it is wanted and/or can be digested.

The confusion of the two roles of parenting and teaching or, to use another language, the unconscious identification of aspects of the parent with aspects of the teacher, is a precondition for any sort of learning. It is what allows schools to play a part in the consolidation or stabilization of gender identities. Though schools' particular contribution to gender may lie in the systematizing and channelling (through examinations, curricular organization and classroom organization) of feelings which are brought into the school settings, these feelings have been fundamentally shaped by relations with parents long before school is entered.

Chapter 5

The Unconscious Meanings of Reading

Reading has enormous significance for the way primary school education is organized, and it is regarded as the basis of most later learning. So it is somewhat surprising that the markedly different attitude and, apparently, aptitude, of boys and girls towards reading and books in general has not become a major educational issue. For gender differences in reading provide the first occasion when schools as institutions have to face gender as a 'problem': how they respond to this problem may set precedents affecting both the course of children's lives and the course of the school in its treatment of gender.

The facts are that girls, on average, read faster, sooner and more fluently than boys. Even more important, possibly, is that they seem to actually enjoy reading, whereas many boys struggle and resist it for as long as possible. Not only is this difference the bane of many parents' and teachers' lives, it has been known about since the early 1960s (Douglas *et al.*, 1968). Then, however, a concern with gender differences was not widespread and boys being up to two years behind girls in reading did not command attention. Gender differences were accepted as developmental and the lower written and verbal levels of boys' academic performance were adjusted to rather than questioned, even to the extent of lowering eleven-plus pass scores for boys to ensure that equal numbers of each sex entered selective schools (Goldstein, 1986). Since the 1960s, a number of surveys (Whitehead, 1977; Gorman *et al.*, 1988; Osmont, 1987; Gipps and Murphy, 1994) have confirmed a continuing gender difference around reading and shown that it persists as children grow older. Although, in terms of sheer ability or performance, it lessens with age and becomes more a matter of a difference in the sort of reading material that boys and girls typically prefer, the difference is definite and persistent. Boys tend to like factual material or comics, whilst girls prefers stories, fiction and romance (Davies and

Brember, 1993). Eventually, most children read, but at the extremes of reading fluency girls feature disproportionately at the top and boys at the bottom. Of course, all this refers to averages. There are many good readers who are boys and a fair number of girls who have to struggle but, overall, the pattern of boys as being tardy at reading is widely reported but not widely understood.

Parents 'tear their hair out' in attempts to encourage their sons to read and the BBC radio programme 'Treasure Islands' helpfully offers listeners a booklist of the books most likely to get boys to read. Teachers worry deeply too, both about the children in their classes who do not read and the possible effect that their efforts to accommodate them might have on the rest of the class. The popularity of the 'real books' approach to teaching reading, preferred by many teachers to reading schemes, is based on the idea that the best way to engage reluctant readers is to start with books on topics in which they already have some interest, and may be seen as a response to the problem of getting boys in mixed classes to read as well as girls. The general predominance of boys among those having reading difficulties is reflected, not just in higher rates of referral to special learning units, but in the titles of articles such as Helen Bromley's (1993) 'At last he's looking at the words' and in the disproportionate use of boys to illustrate points in books aimed at helping teachers such as *The Strugglers* (Martin, 1989). The Dyslexia Association is one of the most energetic of educational pressure groups and, though not explicitly a pressure group for boys' education, the fact that the majority of dyslexic children are male makes it, de facto, into one.

As with all learning difficulties, the strategies and solutions found to overcome problems can have long-term implications, especially for the range of careers that can be considered. A colleague of mine, who had suffered from dyslexia as a child and still read relatively slowly, suggested that he had perhaps unconsciously chosen to work in medicine rather than history, in which he had taken his first degree, because articles in medical journals were a lot shorter to read and to write. And I surely cannot be the only teacher in higher education to have noticed a gender difference in the way that students relate to many of the tables which appear, at least in social science books? Whereas female students tend to read the text, and often avoid looking at tables or graphs, men seem to prefer and concentrate on tables and graphs rather than text. Both strategies, of course, risk missing something, but each suggests a preferred and a less preferred way of taking in information.

At the institutional level a response to reading differences can set a course for responding to other sex differences. If the gender element in reading is denied and children are just viewed as 'good' or 'poor' readers it may make it harder to design effective implementation strategies and/or to raise a general consciousness of gender later on. And if there was a more widespread recognition and open adjustment to the gendered differences in performance at different ages, a lot of educationally based anxiety might be removed. For example, if parents generally knew that boys tended to be two years behind girls in language work and reading, and their sons were compared only to other boys rather than to all children of the same age, they might become a lot more relaxed about their child's progress.

Whilst word-processing and dictaphones may help some dyslexic or dysgraphic children overcome their reading and writing difficulties, and more active or problem-focused strategies of teaching may anyway be desirable, a difficulty with reading cannot be totally circumvented. Individual avoidance strategies are clearly not a general solution; far better would be a deeper understanding of the origins of this gender difference. But avoidance strategies prompt the questions of, first, what exactly it is that is being avoided when a child refuses to read and, second, are the obstacles that boys and girls face different? If they are, then what they avoid and how they avoid may also be different. But before the issue of unconscious obstacles can be addressed the more common explanations of what it means to read and write and why gender seems to affect the process need to be explored.

Conventional Explanations of Gender and Reading

The most orthodox approach to reading and gender differences is the developmental one. It is fairly well established that girls have superior levels of fine motor control and that this enhances their writing skills. There are also hearing differences between boys and girls which affect learning to read and differences in the capacity for visual imagery (McGuiness, 1985). Apparently, girls can perceive sound better than boys at lower levels and this too is one of the factors which leads them to read better. Developmentally, boys have the edge on girls in terms of visual imagery in three dimensions and a better memory for object relations in space. Yet, with all these aptitudes, it is not clear how much the measured differences can be accounted for by the innate skills, and how much by differences in the social experience each gender is offered.

A recent overview by Joan Swann (1992) of research into the differences in aptitude or preference for language-based work from a social constructionist perspective offers three broad types of explanation. The most popular account of the lead in reading that girls enjoy in primary schools tends to be some version of modelling or of the 'feminized classroom' such as that offered by Patricia Sexton (1974). As most primary school teachers are female, so the argument goes, it is easier and more natural for girls to fit in, to identify with and copy the teacher and, in this way, to gain approval and reinforcement. Girls' superior verbal and reasoning skills are explained by a 'girl-friendly' environment made up of women teachers who find it easy to sympathize with them, as illustrated so openly and honestly by Vivian Gussin Paley (1984). Girls thus flourish, enjoying school work and getting confirmation of their abilities at both unconscious and conscious levels, whilst boys fit in less well, find that their activities cause them more often to fall foul of the teacher and set off on a rockier subconscious road. Boys, it is suggested, are put off reading because both genders perceive reading and writing as feminine and passive. It is an activity that fits in well with the prevailing ideas of feminine identity, but is at odds with the active, doing, practical stress of masculine identities.

As the main task of primary school education is to establish easy and confident reading, if the whole milieu is even only slightly disadvantageous to boys, then the fact that a fair proportion of primary school boys are hesitant or reluctant readers should come as no surprise. The only problem with this argument is the evidence that shows how much teachers and schools bend over backwards to accommodate boys' needs. Content analyses of books and reading schemes show that boys' interests are promoted and favoured far more than girls', and observational studies show that attention, verbal and visual, is drawn again and again to boys rather than girls in mixed classrooms. Yet boys still, on average, lag behind girls of the same age in reading. It is boys who make up the majority of pupils receiving 'special needs' attention and, when it is not behavioural problems that land them in this category, it is their difficulties with reading.

Swann's second type of explanation is that the content of much of the reading material used in schools is simply of poor quality. She cites research which found that when a particular effort was made to use exciting content, often specifically to attract boys, the enjoyment and facility in reading it improved for both sexes (though girls, it seemed, were less handicapped by dull books than boys). Her third form of explanation rests on the somewhat ambiguous research on achievement. It is ambiguous because although a female tendency to underestimate their ability and a gendered pattern of attributing success or failure (Deaux, 1977) has often been used to explain girls' failure to continue with science subjects or their tendency to 'play safe' with their choices, it does not fit the reading picture. Swann gets nearer to an anxiety-based explanation when she uses Barbara Licht and Carol

Dweck's (1983) research to explain why girls stick with what they know they can manage, that is, with language-based work, and uses this to explain their 'dominance' in language-based subjects. This line of argument gets qualified support from Janet White (1986) who suggests that girls' very facility with words is part of their educational downfall. The puzzle of why girls' early academic success does not lead to their being sponsored by the educational system is explained because, on the one hand, schools take literary skills for granted when displayed by females whilst, on the other hand, this early success leads girls to cease to compete in other areas. Along with other social constructionist theories this type of explanation has probably been the most elaborated and influential. For older pupils what it means to be 'a reader' or 'a writer' has been explored and linked to dominant images of femininity and masculinity in which the activities of reading and writing are but part and parcel of a series of complex negotiations over sex and power that just happen to be taking place in the classroom (Walkerdine, 1981; Moss, 1989).

Theories of Reading

In fact, in recent years, literary criticism has been rather taken up with demonstrating how complex or impossible the acts of reading and writing are and how the relationships between the author and the reader, or between the book and its apparent subject matter, are far from simple. In varying degrees, the reader is viewed as active, almost a collaborator with the author, whilst the author may be denied credit or 'authorship' for what he or she has produced. The boundaries between people and between books are, increasingly, viewed as fluid, and a notion of 'intertextuality' used to stress that all reading is done within a context and with constant cross-references to other books and other readings.

Yet, at the same time that the reading 'subject' seems to be 'disappearing' or 'fragmenting' there is a growing interest in the human need to communicate and in a 'narrative impulse' to tell stories or interpret one's own life (Bruner, 1990; Polanyi, 1985) which at least focuses attention back on what or who it is that does the telling. Stories, however they are written or told, make us sensitive both to what is said and how it is said and, from this perspective, though 'texts' are not always written, the very physical nature of pens, paper, print and word-processors have also become more important. Though what it means to read or write, and how to do it in the light of theories of reading, has become a huge area of scholarship which lies well beyond the scope of this book, the general 'deconstructionist' trend and concern with different forms of literacy has made it much easier to deal with the symbolism of books and reading and has allowed in a wider range of psychological ideas including psychoanalytical ones. In part this is a continuation of an older debate in literary and art criticism about whether writing, or indeed any form of art, is a representation of the external world or a consequence of an inner need of the artist to displace some form of primitive impulse. But it is also represented in the growing interest in the emotional meanings of myths, stories and fairy tales for children (Bettelheim, 1978; Rustin and Rustin 1987; Rose, 1984).

Reading clearly requires a lot of psychological energy, or desire, to sit still in the first place and then to focus on the words, to allow them in and, ultimately, to shift imaginatively into the world of the book. A strange activity, on the borderline between being conscious and unconscious, reading requires attentiveness, but also a capacity to screen out many of the other distracting events that go on around one all the time. To be an effective reader we have to be able to read easily and unconsciously (i.e. not by saying the words to ourselves), yet we have to be conscious enough to take in and think about the content of what we read. It involves straddling the boundary and being open to association and connection. For reading is not just a mechanical decoding of marks on paper, it is a negotiation, an engagement. Its outcome is not predetermined.

Seen from this perspective it is fairly obvious that relationships and their characteristic forms might hold the key to the whole process. Some of these relationships will be real ones, but some will be internalized, fantasy-based ones. As Bruno Bettelheim and Karen Zelan (1982) observed in *On Learning to Read*, the meaning of what one reads is affected by both the feelings that are brought to the text and the feelings aroused by it which arise from the experience of relationships. Bettelheim then ventures that when children 'misread' they are changing the text to suit their inner purposes. This is part of an age-specific tendency to actively manipulate things and is wholly in accord with a developmental stage. Bettelheim and Zelan therefore urge that non-reading be understood as a response to being *made* to read in a way that 'contradicted the needs that [the child] had tried to express in their misreading'. By forcing a child to read, they warn, we go against that child's 'vital interests'. However, Bettelheim and Zelan do not say very much either about these vital interests or the sex difference in reading patterns to which they are related.

Ideally, a theory which explained the gender difference in reading would link the perceptual/cognitive dimensions with the social and emotional ones. Such a theory might well start with a distinction between reading and books, for books are objects to be handled and manipulated as well as to trigger electrical impulses in the brain, or become the occasion for measuring hand/ eye coordination. They are not only things to be read, to prop open doors with, to be torn up or made into presents, they are the repositories of individual and social meaning and it is in the unconscious meaning of reading and books that the gender difference lies (though most of these meanings are a million miles away from the general tone of primary schools).

In all the material still to be discussed, ideas of sexuality are central and clearly in conflict with the prevailing 'niceness' of primary school pedagogy. For example, one paper argues that books can symbolize the mother's body and that the energy for reading comes from a sublimation of oral and anal drives whilst another argues, yet again, that reading is tied up with separation. If boys have to 'dis-identify' from their mothers in ways that are more painful and more profound than for girls it should come as little surprise that reading can become the occasion for all sorts of unconscious conflicts and inhibitions.

Psychoanalytical Approaches to Reading and Writing

Psychoanalysts are typically interested only in the inner life, not in social institutions unless they come into a particular analysis. As a consequence, not many psychoanalysts have concerned themselves with education. Exceptionally, Anna Freud (1931) gave a series of lectures about psychoanalysis explicitly for teachers; however, she made no mention of the sex differences that she and her audience would be familiar with from their everyday work and experience – possibly because sex differences were not thought to be very important at the time. Binet, after all, had found sex differences right from the start when he began to measure intelligence, but chose to disregard them and combine the scores for each sex (McGuiness, 1985).

It was Melanie Klein's reshaping of psychoanalysis by extending it to children that showed how central gender (and anxiety) were to unconscious meanings of school tasks, and how each related to psychosexual development. Her basic position was that all learning rested on sublimation and that anxiety was one of the primary affects. Schools demanded the repression of libidinal energy which was then available to be channelled into other activities. Hence most of what goes on in schools, for individuals, can be traced back to the progress of their inhibitions, and most of the sex differences in schooling can similarly be traced to the different ways that girls and boys face the Oedipal situation. According to Klein, a boy has to abandon a 'passive feminine attitude, which had hitherto been open to him, in order to put forth his activity'. He has got to act like a man. As she puts it in a footnote to a discussion of the dream of a 13-year-old,

> The maternal significance of dais and also of desk and slate and everything that can be written upon, as well as the penis-meaning of penholder, slate pencil and chalk, and of everything with which one can write, became so evident for me in this and other analyses and was so constantly confirmed that I consider it to be typical. (Klein, 1923)

It is the perennial problem of all psychoanalytic accounts that without clinical and contextual material the interpretations offered can seem, not typical, but absurdly stereotypic and facile. However, it perhaps does not require too much faith to accept that most ordinary children have a profound interest in sexuality, in lavatorial humour, humiliation and magic, and that boys express these interests in a somewhat different way to girls. Sara Delamont's (1989, 1991) structural analyses of the scarey stories told by children to each other about school transfers suggest how the fears and preoccupations become culturally encoded and institutionalized. She lists the main themes of the stories as 'bogwashes', violent gangs, weird or sexually perverse teachers, the supernatural and humiliation, and she reports that whilst both sexes hear and relay the stories, each also knew that the stories were really 'about' and were meant for boys. As a 'cultural form' the scarey story acknowledges that the school, as microcosm of society, is a dangerous place for boys and demands of them greater changes. For all the supposed importance placed on doing well at school academically, physical strength and an unambiguous masculinity are what really count. These stories, like other contemporary myths such as those described by Marina Warner in her Reith Lectures (Warner, 1994), have the power to frighten both young boys and young girls because they mix residual fears derived from infancy with the real fear of growing up in a hostile world. Each order of fear resonates with the other and, for those for whom the future looks most frightening, one response is to resist growing up – exactly what a lot of boys do, though we call it 'late development' or a case of boys' 'maturing' later than girls.

Why they resist or develop later makes most sense in terms of their unconscious drives for instinctual gratification. This, of course, was Bettelheim's point about 'vital interests' and is the wisdom of teachers who recognize that learning cannot be forced, but has to go at the pace of the child. Though now somewhat out of fashion, the ideas of child-centredness and 'reading readiness' are practical expressions of this. Children will learn when it suits their inner life to do so. When they choose to read and what they choose will centre on moments and themes which reflect the fantasies of their stage of development (latency, pre-puberty, etc.) (Friedlander, 1958).

Though concerned with adults' reading rather than with children's, if the ideas floated in James Strachey's (1930) 'The Unconscious Determinants of Reading' are at all convincing they may be applied just as readily to children and their relation to books and reading. Taking as his starting point many of the common phrases or metaphors used to describe books and reading such as being a 'voracious' reader, or 'devouring' a book, which might be considered 'unwholesome', 'indigestible', 'stodgy' or 'strong meat', he suggests that the energy used for reading draws on the sublimation of unconscious oral and anal drives. His examples show the emotional preconditions of reading particularly clearly. As he points out, when we talk of books in this way we show traces of oral pleasure or distaste. The intense absorption and interest in a book is akin to the behaviour of an infant enjoying its meal, and the fact that many adults and children settle to read with a cup of cocoa, a whisky, a pipe or a bag of sweets is no coincidence. Similarly, reading in bed at night is a sort of 'nightcap': it induces sleep because of its near equivalence with oral gratification. The analogy is pushed further still with the suggestion that 'the smooth, uninterrupted enjoyment that characterises the mental states of the novel reader or cinema goer ... suggests ... that their nourishment is liquid and that they are sucking it in' (Strachey, 1931, p. 325). Of course the analogy has its limits, as not all reading is of this sort, just as not all oral experiences are benign and gentle; but such an approach totally changes how reading and gender differences may be thought about.

The second stage of oral, libidinal gratification is a more ambivalent psychological state, as it encompasses both pleasure and the capacity to inflict pain. Strachey argues that it can be detected in reading behaviour by the common practice of mouthing words when reading. Talking and reading are connected, but not the same. Talking is a method of expelling words, whilst reading is the opposite, a matter of taking something in, of 'eating' another person's words. Difficulties with reading are tied more closely to the ambivalence of the second oral phase in which, though the words/food may be savoured some of the time, they are also fodder for more sadistic and destructive impulses. Digesting the word/food gets difficult, they are hard to swallow/ read and have to be chewed/re-read time and time again.

If ingestion is one of the earliest pleasures that gets sublimated into reading then, by the same means, so too does that other early pleasure, defecation. Turning from the aim of reading to its object Strachey draws on Freud's statement that books and paper are female symbols and on Ernest Jones' view that printed matter is a symbol of faeces. He argues (partly by appealing to our knowledge of the common habit of reading on the lavatory, often as a method of relieving constipation) for seeing a connection between eating and defecating which lies at the root of all reading and reading difficulty. The author excretes his thoughts and embodies them in the printed book; the reader takes them and, after chewing them over, incorporates them into himself (p. 329). The coprophagic case is given another twist when Strachey suggests that faeces can also represent the father or his penis and the wish to eat them can convey feelings of rivalry, hostility, destructiveness as well as guilt at so doing. Disgust at the fantasy can thus express both the negative feelings and fears of retribution for harbouring them. As copulation can be unconsciously equated with insemination, Strachey then speculates that a person might feel 'feminine' and wish to be in the mother's place taking in the faeces/penis; though, as ever, the possibilities are more complex and these fantasized children inside the mother could be resented and envied and then, in fantasy, annihilated or eaten.

Loss, Separation, Gender and Reading

If Strachey's ideas about what books can symbolize seem bizarre, a less challenging version may be Daniel Pennac's (1994) *Reads Like a Novel*. This starts with the point that books are not only things to read, but to prop open doors with, tear up and make into presents. In everyday life many of the fantasized uses suggested by Strachey are indeed executed. In this book, billed as a 'manifesto' of readers' rights, Pennac manifestly trumpets the readers' right to *use* the books at will: to skip, to browse, to read aloud or not at all, to read 'trash' and to leave books unfinished. Implicitly, it builds on Strachey's account of reading as affected by unconscious processes and of books as repositories of individual and social meaning, and forms a bridge between Strachey and Klein on the one hand, and Chodorow on the other.

Though the book is clearly based on the idea that reading, or rather non-reading, is about separation, relationships and the unconscious meanings of books, there is not a single reference to psychoanalysis. It is simply a plea to parents to stop pressuring their children to read. In making his case, Pennac stresses the materiality of books and their role as the symbols of love and hate and relationships. A book was 'an object that's thick, compact, dense and bruising ... a timeless lump. It is boredom made palpable'. As a consequence, when reading was made into a task, the book itself would become unforgiving and unresponsive:

> The lines jammed with words compressed between miniscule margins, black paragraphs heaped one on top of other, and here and there the oasis of some inverted commas, indicating the charity of a dialogue. But the other character doesn't reply. Followed by a block of twelve pages! Twelve pages of black ink! Shitting, fucking hell. (Pennac, 1994, p. 12)

Pennac's mission was to make parents realize that their children's 'failure' to read was a form of mourning for the time when parents still read *to* their children and for the lost intimacy of that period. Then, the parent and the book had been the same and, because being read to in bed was so close and loving, its termination was felt as an especially cruel rejection. Reading on one's own, or being told to do so, was quite different and carried other meanings, the most important of which was that it revived or repeated the separation crisis for boys. Though Pennac makes no reference to it, his thesis is almost identical to Chodorow's, namely that there is a crisis about separation, gender and childrearing in western culture. The gender element is implicit rather than explicit, for though Pennac is clearly preoccupied with boys, their reading and their relationships with their fathers, the reader of this book is left to infer it from the continuous use of 'He' for all children or teenagers and the sparse references to girls.

This singularity is not surprising in a book so personal, and it comes through in almost every sentence.

> As I think back on it now, as insomnia takes hold, the ritual of the bedtime story had something of the quality of prayer to it: every evening while he was little, at the foot of his bed, the hour set and the gestures sacrosanct. A sudden armistice after the rumpus of the day, a reunion unaffected by contingencies; the moment of rapt silence before the first words of the story, when our voice would at last be restored to itself; and the liturgy of the episodes. Yes, the bedtime story filled the most beautiful role which prayer has to offer, the most disinterested, the least gain-seeking, which involves mankind uniquely: the forgiveness of trespass. No fault would be confessed, no attempt would be made to gain a portion of eternity. There would be a moment of communion, between us, involving the absolution of the text and a return to the only paradise which counts,

that of intimacy. Without knowing it, we were discovering one of the essential roles of stories, and on larger scale, of art in general, which is to impose a truce upon human combat. (Pennac, 1994, p. 24)

And, later,

sending him to bed without telling him his story meant turning his day into an unbearably dark night. It meant taking leave of him without first having reunited with him – an intolerable punishment both for him and for us. (Pennac, 1994, p. 30)

In telling the parent how much he had betrayed his son, Pennac points out that when parents read books to their children they become the book and the listening child becomes the ideal reader. Consequently, when parents nag their children they destroy the relationship and turn themselves from being a story-teller to being an accountant.

Repetition reassures, it is proof of intimacy. It's the very breath of intimacy, and its just this breath he needs to rediscover
'Again'
'Again, again is a simple way of saying "We must really love one another, you and I, to find satisfaction in a single story, repeated endlessly!"' To re-read is not to repeat oneself, it's to give a sign, constantly renewed, of a tireless love. (Pennac, 1994, p. 50)

Pennac (1994) pursues his idea of the link between good reading and love and observes:

the greatest things we've read are usually owed to someone dear to us. And it's to someone dear to us that we'll speak of them first.' (p. 81) ... Anyone who reads out loud to you is telling you loudly that you can become worthy of the book being read. He's really making you a gift of reading. (p. 90)

Again, without any mention of Freud or Winnicott, Pennac demonstrates that books are symbols of people and what happens between them. As an example he explains why the mistreatment of books by others is so upsetting – because of the confusion between books and the parts of people that they may unconsciously symbolize. When we finish reading something it becomes part of ourselves, especially if we like it. Sometimes, if the book we are reading is borrowed, we may have difficulties returning it, not because we are thieves, but because there is a 'sliding of property' or a 'transfer of substance'.

> Few objects awaken in the way books do a feeling of absolute ownership. When they fall into our hands, books become our slaves – yes, slaves since they're living matter, yet slaves no one would dream of emancipating, since they're made out of dead leaves. As such they are subjected to the worst sorts of treatment, resulting from the most passionate of loves or the most frightful of furies (p. 140).... We submit books to every kind of abuse (p. 141).... What a wound, every time there's a sight of a page with its corner folded ... those rings, those traces of bread and jam, those spots of sun tan oil! And to think I leave my thumb print all over you (p. 140).

They are, in Winnicott's terms, 'transitional objects'.

The experience of reading flows, almost imperceptibly, from and into early relationships and the experiences of love, giving, merging, separating from parents, loneliness and establishing a separate identity. Reading alone marks a major shift, it demands emotional maturity and self-confidence which generally comes later. As another writer, Antonia Byatt, describes it:

> Reading is a private activity and entails a private relationship between two people, reader and writer. It takes place over time, unless the reader rejects the book. Spoken language can take short cuts, take cues from the respondents' face or situation. Written language is addressed to someone unknown – it makes an imagined world, a sustained argument, a passionate plea, out of one person's inner life, and offers it to another separate person to experience and think about. It is a matter of what used to be called the inner life.... The relations between feeling, thinking and imagining are not the same in any other art form. (Byatt, 1992)

Gender, Loneliness and Separation

Reading is a process that depends upon a secure sense of self; it demands a capacity to be alone, and this may be harder for boys because of their socialization. Paradoxically, the stress on independence, as part of the core of male identity, has led to norms and behaviour which rest on a radical (and often emotionally premature) 'dis-identification' or separation of boys from their mothers and to a clear double standard. If we follow Bettelheim in remembering that reading is about feeling, not decoding, then a clear path opens up towards seeing how sex differences in reading may lie in the unconscious.

When children of both sexes are largely reared by women, boys are progressively expected to acquire the values and behaviour of men. This is no easy task as in most homes men are not around as much as women are for young boys to learn from, at least through the easiest form of learning, which is by identification. Hence, right from the start, the very nature of learning the male gender identity in western society is more difficult, more abstract and more precarious. Though the long-term social gains may be considerable, the immediate experience is of loss, rejection and anxiety. Coping mechanisms for dealing with the loss may work in the short run, but they too are increasingly viewed as being emotionally disabling for men and boys in the long run. Girls, by contrast, are allowed, if they want, to remain in a state of identification with their mothers. They are not required to 'dis-identify' or to model themselves on someone of whom they may have little knowledge and contact. Childhood, at least early on, seems easier for them.

Chodorow drew directly on object relations theory and the assumption that early relationships provided the pattern for later ones. Women continued to accept the role of mothers because their identities had been constructed around an unbroken identification with their own mothers. They had never had to disavow their closeness with their mothers and hence they found work, paid and unpaid, which required them to be sensitive to the needs, thoughts and feelings of other people relatively easy. They had not been obliged to develop a different way of being, or re-construct their identity through separateness, as boys were, and their sense of being able to merge with others could, in terms of parenting, be an asset. Men, by contrast, found parenting and other intimate relations difficult because they had been forced to define themselves in terms of separation. Years of coping with what was felt as a rejection by their mothers and getting on with the prescribed masculinity did not leave them well placed to re-assume relations which depended on sensitivity, indeterminacy and a tolerance for a blurred boundary between self and other.

In terms of reading, girls' superiority fits easily into the account of childrearing where closeness with a mother is encouraged and permitted and continues longer for girls. Girls, on this model, read well because intimacy is allowed whereas boys do not because they are 'weaned' more forcefully. This is not just a matter of practical weaning from the breast, but of being required to be independent and of not too openly enjoying contact with the mother. Yet, as we know, reading schemes which involve parents are the most successful, so it requires no great leap of the imagination to see that reading progress might be closely tied to relations with parents. But this is only a start. It is not just sitting and being cuddled while being read to at the age of 4, 5, 6 or 7 that matters, it is what books can symbolize and the broader meaning of separation.

Parting and loss are unavoidable throughout life yet, paradoxically, they are the bases of emotional growth. The question is how we cope with them and whether we view alternatives and substitutes as opportunities or threats. Schooling, as a realm of experience, constantly repeats or echoes these early experiences by moving us on from topic to topic, class to class, teacher to teacher at a pace that is rarely our own. The now unfashionable idea of 'reading readiness' was rather more sensitive to these sorts of emotional undercurrents which strike me as ever more influential as I watch in my own family a certain resistance to learning in school and to ever being hurried; these two things seem to me to be linked.

Yet, except in the crudest form of behaviourism, experiences are never repeated exactly, they are only ever approximations to past experiences, roughly matched and always in need of interpretation and reinterpretation. At root the issue is not how similar or different teaching is from parenting, though one is obviously grafted onto the other, but how teachers encapsulate, challenge and transform experiences already laid down, and in so doing affect the capacity to learn. In this case learning to read, as the first and most important task of primary schooling, is critical. However, there are other aspects of parenting that infuse teaching. The more we delve into the experience of teaching and learning the closer it gets to feeding and early relations with caretakers, who are usually women. Feeding and learning display some similar patterns and may offer a clue to the reading difficulties that so many boys have. As mothers generally spend more time than fathers in feeding children and in reading to them it is possible that if struggle, conflict and resistance have already become features of the relationship, as a result of the feeding experience, then they are likely to be part of the attempt to teach reading too. This is not to paint all mothers as locked in conflict with their children, but the experience of children refusing to do something for their mothers when they will do the same task for someone else is very common and suggests that it is not the task but who is requiring it that is important.

At an unconscious level it is possible that new experiences, be they of food or school tasks, are approached in similar ways, with fear and dread, or with enthusiasm and excitement. If books are food and the first food is milk from a mother's breast then, if books and papers are also symbols of the female body, reading and writing may stand unconsciously for ways of relating to that body. If there is even a grain of truth in this, boys are caught in a trap. Just as they are expected to detach themselves or 'dis-identify' from their mothers they are invited to do exactly the work which subconsciously means defiling their mothers.

At a purely anecdotal level I have long been aware of how much easier my daughter finds it to get absorbed in activities on her own and how much my son, even though is he older, seems to need my or his father's presence. Reading and writing certainly seems for him a more lonely and much less attractive experience. Moreover, my daughter, who was keen to read and write from an early age, was equally keen to scribble over books and walls. My son, though not necessarily more careful of property, has never scribbled in books or on the walls. The books and the wall are much more 'no-go' areas for him, and very possibly hold different unconscious meanings. There is not the same demand on our daughter to be different and separate, hence separation for her is more chosen. It does not seem like a rejection and is therefore less threatening. In sociohistorical terms, literacy, and in particular the printed word, is associated with individualism and the growth of the self-defining subject (Leed, 1980). It has a similar association with individual growth. The child who will not read or write, who does not know what to say or who wants to be told what to say, is also staking his claim to be still part of the parent.

Gender and Writing

Though Strachey does not consider it, something similar to the processes he describes about reading occur with writing too. Young boys tend to find it hard to put pen to paper whilst girls have less difficulty and can cover pages and pages with ease. Paradoxically, the opposite holds with computers. Though the sex difference is not as marked when computers are used for word-processing as when they are used for games, computers do seem to enable quite a lot of 'blocked boys' to at least write something. Many of the boys and male students that I am familiar with have problems both with the act of writing (their handwriting is much clumsier and less neat than that of most girls) and with the notion of composition. They write as little as possible, with great effort, and tend to say that they do not know what to write or do not have 'enough to say'. Even when one asks a question which is easily answered, they still cannot write it down and say, incredulously, 'Will that be alright ... is that really OK?'.

Very often boys fail to see the point of writing at all, or find that the choice of word is so significant that they can hardly do it. When this happens, the inner need for precision and accuracy is so great that no word is better than some word which is felt as the wrong word, and it is as if many of them have a 'writer's block'. Of course, a child who has never been able to write freely is not the same as an adult who once could but then finds that they can no longer write, but the source of the blockages may have something in common and, as Adam Phillips (1993) has recently argued, obstacles or blocks are extremely interesting in their own right. Playfully transforming Winnicott's object-relations into obstacle-relations he suggests that obstacles are important because they are a clue to desire: they perform the crucial role of maintaining a connection with the desired object. As he puts it, if you know what the obstacle is then you know what is desired and what is desired is the key to virtually all subsequent behaviour. An obstacle then, is a form of transitional object or transitional space because it keeps at bay what Phillips calls the two 'fundamental terrors', namely, absolute merging or absolute loss. As a transitional object, the obstacle makes a place where experience can happen.

Zachary Leader (1991) comes at these issues from a similar direction. Though he is concerned only with adults, not children, his general thesis is that all blocked writers suffer from a failure to negotiate rival or competing claims. These may take the form of a conflict between inner and outer, or between primary and secondary process, between emergence and embeddedness, between subject and object, male and female, defusion and merger, written and oral, or independence versus incorporation. In all these instances the task, made concrete by the demand to write, is to negotiate the polarities. However, on occasion the illusion that this is possible will simply break down, or one of the claims will dominate the other.

Though gender is not his prime concern, the use Leader makes of Plato's criticism of writing may be of a more gendered cast than he realizes. The reasons Plato gave for distrusting writing, and poetry in particular, was that it was a slippery, deceptive medium which relied on metaphor. It damaged both those who wrote and those who read, whereas oral culture and philosophy which were based on direct communication were more truthful and therefore more honourable. They dealt with evidence, not trickery. Writing played with words, twisting them to mean something else, and it had to be opposed. It gave power, the power of deceit. Whilst Leader stresses that it is the need to deal with rivalrous claims that paralyses and disables the writer, it is implicit in his book, which mainly deals with male writers, that male problems with writing lie in their early experiences of Oedipal rivalry and separation. If socially required activities, such as the demand for literacy, encapsulate these early experiences at an unconscious level, it is not surprising that complying is both difficult and intense for the male, whether he is a professional writer or just a young boy.

Often students treat writing as a matter of second-guessing what the tutor wants, rather than expressing their own thoughts and the product of their reading. It is as if, at the unconscious level, the task is to make contact rather than to launch out on their own. And that contact has to be made prior to writing, not as a consequence of it as professional writers claim. For many boys the request to write some form of prose, even a diary, is felt as something supremely abstract. They have to imagine the unimaginable rather than describe what is in front of them. This difficult task of abstraction parallels or crystallizes the general pattern of boys' socialization into a masculine identity as more abstract than girls' socialization into a feminine identity. Once it is achieved, the masculine preference for abstraction is championed as superior to other forms of intellectual work which, especially when associated with women, is a reminder of what has been lost. Thus fiction, especially that which deals with emotions and relationships, is denigrated and avoided or treated as inferior by many boys partly because it is capable of more than one interpretation.

Chapter 6

Curricula and Transitional Objects

Many readers of Winnicott find it easy to accept the idea of transitional objects when illustrated by examples of babies being attached to teddy bears and blankets as comforting substitutes for a parent, but understandably baulk when the concept is extended to explain all artistic production and consumption. Television watching, hi-fis and jacuzzis perhaps (Silverstone, 1993; Csikszentmihalyi and Rochberg-Halton, 1981; Young, 1989), but even applying it to books and reading as the last chapter did can strain credulity. But I want to go further and argue, first, that academic disciplines such as English, maths, physics or computer studies are a form of transitional object and, second, that viewing them in this way gives us a better chance of understanding the marked gender divisions in subject choice that appear first around GCSE and then even more so at 'A' level and in higher education. In the next chapter, I suggest that this stereotyping and polarization of subject choice is tied to gender-specific patterns of psychological development and identity formation in which anxiety plays a large part, but in this chapter I concentrate on the meaning of a discipline or subject and aim to show how this grows out of the process of teaching. All of which is preliminary to suggesting that when children move from primary schools, where teaching is person-based, to secondary schools, where it is subject-based, the preconditions of learning are altered which, in turn, affects the sex stereotyping and subject choices which characterize the later stages of education.

Teaching as a Transitional Space

Exactly how teaching leads to learning is unknown. As the car sticker which proclaims 'If you can read this – thank a teacher' points out, there is a link, but exactly what that link is is hard to establish. Without teachers much learning would not take place, but even with them it is not assured, and learning is certainly not tied to formal education, as Ivan Illich's *Deschooling Society* (1971) made patently clear. When teaching is done well, it is particularly difficult to identify and disentangle the contribution of the teacher from the contribution of the pupil or student. For, as with the baby, there is an important confusion or illusion which leads the pupil to experience as their own achievement some of the effort of the teacher. This illusion can be very debilitating for teachers and is one of the reasons why teaching can be such a depressing occupation. The better teaching is done, the harder it is to see one's product, and it takes a fair degree of emotional maturity to be able to bear this for years on end. But this blurring of what comes from the teacher and what comes from the student is also the reason why teaching may be understood as a 'transitional space'.

Daniel Lindley (1993) describes this process in a teaching manual which embodies his experience as a Jungian analyst and director of a teacher training programme:

> the goal of teaching is not to teach 'well' ... in fact trying to do so is actually a problem, an over involvement of ego ... teaching too dramatically takes up all the space in the classroom ... [it is] to create a situation in which, at a certain moment, the student, who has been working, struggling, and pondering suddenly says, with a mingled sense of elation and loss: 'I knew that. I knew that all along'. Successful teaching, in other words, has to do with what is already in the student. (Lindley, 1993, p. 12)

This model of the good teacher, or the teacher working at their best, is quite explicitly derived from Winnicott's description of the mother and infant, for Lindley urges that the aim of teaching is to be 'the right teacher at the right time' and that both the curriculum and the teacher need to *resonate* with the pupil's inner states. As a Jungian, Lindley suggests that the trick for teachers is to recognize an 'inner child' in themselves and ally that inner child with the inner adult that is in the pupil, as well as with the actual child/pupil, and that the way to do this is through a form of shared play. The teacher has to identify with some part of the unknowing, excited child and share a journey of discovery. Lindley's *This Rough Magic* advises intending teachers how to pose questions, how to plan classes and how to avoid stress and burn-out. All of his very sensible advice is based on recognizing that teaching is about unconscious as much as conscious communication, and that the teacher and the subject material that they teach have to become, or operate like, a transitional object if they are to be effective. However, this cannot be formulaic. We cannot teach teachers how to be transitional objects, because phenomena of this sort are chosen, not imposed, as much schooling is. Whatever it is that serves the purpose is unique and only works for the child who has endowed it as special. My son's 'Gonky' had no special meaning for his younger sister; and a teacher who had seemed dull when she taught him seemed excellent only two years later when she taught that younger sister.

To recap for a moment, the idea of transitional objects is that they help an infant to survive the frustrations of infancy and the inevitable, temporary separations from its mother – they are literally a stop-gap. Starting with the child's ability to fantasize or wish for and imagine the breast, or the satisfaction that feeding at the breast can bring, it quickly develops a capacity for illusion (fantasy, imagination or whatever one wants to call it) and can allow itself to find comfort in some substitute that it endows with special properties. As life proceeds we all have to learn to comfort ourselves, and we get into reading, model building, playing computer games, etc., as a way of doing that. The activities are all 'recreations', that is, they recreate pleasure. Though it is a somewhat crude theory of culture, Winnicott thought that the transitional object experience was the template for all subsequent cultural experience. The capacity to be 'taken in', to experience pleasure through symbols, though arrived at on an individual basis, is what makes the later, adult enjoyment of cultural artifacts possible. A sensitivity to meaning starts off as a private and idiosyncratic experience but it gradually becomes social and shared. Just as the baby imposes some order on the world and inner feelings by using comforters so do adults, by listening to music or watching television.

Cultural Experience and Transitional Phenomena

On this model, the role of culture is to shape disorganized, pre-social experience and contain it. This goes as much for those who 'consume' culture as those who produce it: both activities are creative; both involve finding meaning. But, because more attention is normally given to the 'creators' of culture, it is worth exploring how cultural artifacts can be thought of as transitional objects and why they depend on an ambiguity between finding and making. Evelyn Glennie, the percussionist, may illustrate the point. It strikes most people as extraordinary that she is both a leading international musician and profoundly deaf. How, they wonder, can she produce music if she cannot hear it? At what point, when and how does the music enter her? When she reads the score? Through her bones? Before or after she picks up an instrument? The very idea forces us to reconsider the notion of what music is, as well as what is inside a person or outside. Does she hear or invent the sound? There is a real possibility that in her case deafness is the key to her creativity, for she lives more continuously than most of us in that *potential space* that Winnicott (1975) defined as the essential property of *cultural experience.*

For those of us brought up within a western philosophical tradition it is especially difficult to grasp and hold on to ideas which make muddle, liminality or indeterminacy central. But they are essential to the quality of *potential* which, in turn, is necessary for creativity and is a defining feature of a transitional object. Because sharedness and things being simultaneously inside and outside are harder to describe than well-bounded phenomena, those who have grappled with these ideas (Kuhn, 1962; Bourdieu, 1971) have tended to use metaphors such as 'fields' or 'paradigms' to overcome the problem of the unstable location of ideas and the ambiguous nature of the relationship between any one artist, scientist or writer and their public, audience or intellectual community. Kuhn is famous for challenging the cumulative notion of scientific progress and for showing that for bright new ideas to be accepted, there had to be a paradigm shift within the scientific community; whilst Bourdieu argued that artists were always aware of their public and that this imagined relationship was an intrinsic part of the creative act. Writing in the heyday of French structuralism, Bourdieu stressed that a cultural or intellectual field was a system of relations between themes and problems rather like a magnetic one, its structure determined by changing relations rather than fixed positions. Though Bourdieu was less obviously constructionist than Kuhn, both were concerned with the dynamics between the knower and the object of knowledge; both recognized that individuals could not work outside of a community of sorts and that this meant all artistic or intellectual activity was essentially shared.

It is a short step from Kuhn and Bourdieu to Winnicott, for all three were concerned with how fields or subjects came into being and the mutual determination of the subject matter and those who practise it. Each conveys a sense of a chain of being, of creativity coming out of a set of relationships, often unconscious, between people whose imaginative existence may be lightly or firmly grasped, but is always there. By the time the artist or scientist is adult and working professionally their subject or field has become institutionalized and has lost most of the traces it once bore of an originally personal relationship. But it is no coincidence that artists often describe themselves as being merely the vehicle of a muse. They do not know where the ideas come from, only that, in certain states, they are more or less open to them and that they do not 'own' them. These sorts of descriptions fit in well with Winnicott's idea of a relationship as preceding the creative act and with his famous remark claiming that 'there is no such thing as a baby – only a mother and baby in relationship with each other' in which he staked out his claim that in an infant's life mergedness and relationship precede any sense of self and separateness. The 'transitional objects' of infancy were the means to that first sense of individual identity and agency, and cultural artifacts were a means to its maintenance in later life.

It may seem a bit of a leap to claim an academic discipline as transitional object but in the context of choice it makes some sense, though it is far from easy to define exactly what a subject or discipline is. When Tony Becher (1989) was studying the 'academic tribes and territories' of higher education, he found it impossible to separate the domain from those within it, for the 'very nature of being a member of a disciplinary community involves a sense of identity and personal commitment, a way of being in the world, a matter of taking on a cultural frame that defines a great part of one's life'. Becher was interested in professional academics who had made careers out of their subjects, but the same is essentially true for schoolchildren too. Lifestyles are tied up with the choice of subject, and in *Contrary Imaginations* Liam Hudson (1966) found that by the age of 11 children had a clear idea of the dull and boring scientist, married to a frump, stuck in a rut. Though the study was primarily about different thought patterns or 'convergent' and 'divergent' imaginations, it revealed the stereotypes of different subjects held by English schoolboys of the time. By contrast to the scientist, the schoolboys' image of the artist was much more fun: artists' wives were also imagined as more attractive. Stereotypes of this sort show how subjects are containers for feelings as well as symbols of the self which affect the direction that might be taken and whether or not the pupil or student can grow and flourish within it. Being able to see oneself as a scientist, artist or linguist is clearly part of taking up a subject and images of that subject affect whether one can, or wants to, see oneself in those terms.

It may not be very often that we meet people who say that they are uplifted by the theorem or problem that they are working on, in the way that many say music is what makes their life worth living, but they do exist. They are intensely and emotionally involved with their subjects and find them enriching in the way that others find a Bach cello suite or a Goya painting enriching. For much the same reasons academic subjects can also be treated as transitional objects, for they too serve emotional purposes. They can be 'loved' or they can be 'hated'. Either way, they function as containers for inner feelings or as spaces in which creativity can occur. As Becher points out, mathematicians like their work to be described as 'powerful', 'elegant' or even 'parsimonious', historians yearn to be described as 'masterful', physicists to 'discover', engineers to 'invent' and sociologists to be hailed as 'stimulating', 'persuasive' or 'imaginative'. Different disciplines, different forms of praise, but all link feeling to creativity. Just as music was, for Evelyn Glennie, both an emotional experience and a discipline in which she plays and is creative, so are academic subjects for many others.

School Subjects as Transitional Objects

How this works subject by subject is beyond my scope, so a few illustrations will have to do. In *The Mathematical Experience* Davis and Hersh (1981, p. 34) offer a tongue-in-cheek sketch of the ideal mathematician as a man obsessed with his work. Cut off from all but perhaps a dozen specialists and regarding his field as more important than anything else he is incapable of communicating, except with the other twelve. The 'rigorous thought' and accepted or formal procedures which define it contrast with 'intuition' as a mode of thought which is 'plausible or convincing' but does not depend on 'proof'. Being a mathematician involves a commitment to not working intuitively. Though a parody, Davis and Hersh offer their vignette as a way of suggesting that different subjects present distinct opportunities for people of different personalities.

A very similar argument about subject choice and personality was made by Jan Harding and Michael Sutoris (1987) to explain the differential involvement of boys and girls in science and technology. Adapting the ideas of both Nancy Chodorow and Ronald Fairbairn they were perhaps the first to apply an object relations perspective explicitly to subject choice. In their account, it was the relatively early separation from their mothers that, typically, led boys to have a lower tolerance of ambiguity and uncertainty. In order to assuage a personal nightmare, they were inclined, in due course, to choose the relatively clear-cut and controllable subjects of science and technology.

For boys, the effect of being pushed out of a dependent relationship with their mother or other caretaker was equivalent to the failure of the mother to survive, and it was this that promoted separation anxiety. From the boys' (unconscious) point of view emotional dependence on a caretaker is destructive, it leads to vulnerability and a suitable response is to keep emotions inside whilst meeting emotional needs indirectly by controlling and possessing objects as if they were substitutes for the adaptive caretaker (mother). Thus aggressive, taking relationships become a feature of boys' 'object relations' and their choice of academic subject symbolizes their psychological accommodation. The most notorious example of how subjects or fields are gendered through their role as containers for feelings is computer studies, for computing has become actually more masculine as it has developed (Lovegrove and Hall, 1987; Griffiths, 1988). The reasons for this clearly go beyond simple stereotyping or any linkage of computing studies with other subjects such as mathematics which are already highly gendered, and most observers have sought explanation in the realm of emotional meanings.

Sherry Turkle (1980, 1984) has, at various points, described the computer as an 'Evocative Object' or a 'Rorschach' and seen it as a projective medium which 'speaks' to the larger concerns of individuals. She claims that it is powerful because it performs a number of psychological tasks. It offers a unique opportunity to be both alone and not alone. Its predictability is a defence against inner chaos and unpredictability and, for this reason, it is enormously reassuring. For both sexes it offers a chance to build a world in which they are successful, but there are differences in the way that each sex interprets this opportunity which Turkle describes as the difference between 'hard' and 'soft' mastery. Boys' pleasure comes from straight mastery, girls' from putting themselves into a sense of space (for example, as birds). Boys seem especially interested in eliminating bugs, whereas girls tolerate imperfection more readily and are more willing to 'negotiate' a relationship with the computer. They find the idiosyncrasies attractive and, unlike boys, do not insist that the computer does it *their* way.

Turkle herself makes a connection between these patterns and the debate in science about gender and method sparked off by Evelyn Fox Keller's (1983) biography of the biologist, Barbara McClintock. McClintock has stressed that in her experimental work she had a 'feeling for the organism', which she interpreted as a form of fusion with the object of study and which stood in marked contrast to the philosophy of science orthodoxy which prescribed a strict separation between subject and object. Turkle explicitly interprets this in object relations terms describing the computer as sitting:

on many borders; it is a formal system that can be taken up in a way that is not separate from the experience of the self. As such, it may evoke unconscious memories of objects that lie for the child in the uncertain zone between self and not-self. These are objects, like Linus' baby blanket [or] the tattered rag doll ... to which children remain attached even as they embark on the exploration of the world beyond the nursery. Psychoanalytic theorists call these objects 'transitional' because they are thought to mediate between the child's closely bonded relationship with the mother and his or her capacity to develop relationships.... (Turkle, 1984, pp. 117–18)

Because computers, like some other forms of equipment, offer an apparent largesse as well as a sense of control, they have become the prime metaphor for modern life and its contradictions. 'We cede to the computer the power of reason but, at the same time, in defense, our sense of identity becomes increasingly focused on the soul and the spirit in the human machine' (Turkle, 1984, p. 312). However, gender affects the way the computer is used imaginatively as well as practically. For example, in a project on the pace of life I found that when people were asked what object or machine best represented their lives, computers were by far the most popular choice as a symbol of the self, for all ages and both sexes. Yet, whereas men saw themselves as mainframes and used the image to suggest immense under-used power if they spent their days on trivial tasks, women identified with PCs or cursors. What they seemed to identify with was the subversive potential of computers on which others had become dependent: they delighted in imagining how, if pushed too far and hard, they might just scramble the files and mess everything up. It would be too much of a digression at this point to explore if and how feminine pleasure was quintessentially subversive but it is worth noting that others, especially when discussing femininity as 'masquerade', have noted this possibility.

In practical terms computers continue to offer different emotional services. As word-processors they clearly help some people overcome writing blocks and embarrassment about poor handwriting or spelling (and it is boys who have more difficulties in these areas). Good, clean copy is a reward that encourages the reluctant to press on and may even make the words flow for once, though, for a minority, the fear of loss by accidental deletion is insuperable (Lyman, 1984). Loss, and how much of it can be tolerated, is probably the key for both those who do, and those who do not, like computing: but there is another theme based on the emotional meanings of computing that ties in with boys' affinity for computing and their more fraught relationship to writing. Computing and databases have an air of accessibility and public property which contrasts with the notions of privacy which still surround the written word, especially the handwritten word.

Although there are passwords and arrangements to maintain privacy, the need for these is related to the powerful appeal of hacking and of entering other people's data, as well as to the sense of databases as public property per se. The idea that computers offer a symbolic opportunity to enter forbidden territory, and especially territory that might stand for the mother's body (rather like Strachey's books), has become a fashionable explanation of the attraction computer and video games hold for boys and men. Taking a Kleinian approach Gillian Skirrow (1986) proposes that if everything frightening and uncanny is displaced into the inside of the mother's body, the appeal of computer games is that they allow players into the 'maternal cave', and yet keep faith with the idea of that as a dangerous place. She adds that as computers require no particular facility with language they may be even more attractive.

But it is not only computers that can play this important role of reassuring or enabling blocked-up energy to be released. Equipment of all sorts may do it. The writers suffering from writer's block mentioned in the last chapter were often quite obsessive about the exact conditions necessary for them to write, the time, the place, the silence or the music, the pen or the desk, etc. These objects, which get the writer into the right mood, perform exactly the same function as any infantile comforter and work to inhibit or to release energy. Another example of the sustaining quality of equipment might be Rosalind Franklin's X-rays. It was she who discovered the DNA pattern though it was the men in the team, Watson and Crick, who took the Nobel prize. As a woman, her marginalization was not unusual; what *was* unusual was how she stuck her working conditions for as long as she did and in a funny sort of way it may have been her equipment and her relationship with it that enabled her to stay within the project, despite the sexism and the ridicule from her colleagues. Seeing shapes in X-rays is, perhaps, a good metaphor for Winnicott's notion of creativity and the quality that subjects and transitional objects share with each other.

If we turn to the arts and humanities we can find a familiar view of English as the embodiment of, and the opportunity to develop, the deepest personal and social values. In the liberal, Leavisite tradition, English has often been viewed as a vehicle for personal growth. At various points, doing well in it has rested on perceptiveness and sensibility; even empathy and entering into the psyche of the author and/or characters has become a skill to be assessed in the national curriculum. The manner in which a range of personal feelings are tied up with and implicitly encouraged by studying 'English' is evident in the language used to describe some of the tasks. English 'appreciation', like 'music appreciation' invites or evokes a response in the warmer end of the feelings range, unlike 'criticism' which hints at the cooler end. Both are evaluative and may, in practice, come to the same conclusions, but they frame the task and orient the pupil in different directions.

English lessons have a particular scope for giving expression to feeling, and not only because they tend to be more frequent in the timetable and therefore allow more of a relationship to be built up with a teacher. The tasks are more elastic; they allow pupils and teachers space in which to play. An example of how the latitude of the English curriculum and the nature of the material may become a lifeline is given by Bernard Harrison (1986) in his *Sarah's Letters: A Case Study of Shyness*, which shows how a withdrawn teenage girl used the space that was her English lesson to help her resolve a knot of family-based dilemmas. What started out as an exercise on Macbeth grew into a correspondence that went on for several years, and in which 'Sarah' worked on and through her feelings about friends and family. However special and flexible Harrison may have been as a teacher, he makes it clear that the letters and the emotional growth would not have happened in another lesson, and himself points to the relevance of object relations in understanding what happened. It was the material, English literature, that was as enabling just as much as he the teacher was as a person. Unconsciously, teacher and subject had become interchangeable.

Of course, not everyone views English as a straightforward avenue to personal growth, and feminists especially have criticized the masculinist bias of English, the narrowness of the canon, and the deceptiveness of the personalist discourse (Gilbert, 1990). And not all subjects encourage personal growth at all. Against the somewhat romantic view painted by Harrison has to be set the fact that many children find certain subjects absolutely loathsome and lessons become a place of terror and mental paralysis. Indeed, this is recognized by many teachers who adopt fear reduction as their primary teaching strategy. Mathematics and language are the subjects which seem to cause most anxiety, and a secondary literature of books with titles such as *Do You Panic about Maths? Coping with Maths Anxiety* (Buxton, 1981) or *Relearning Mathematics* (Frankenstein, 1989) has grown up around them.

Choice, Anxiety and the Curriculum

Although going through subjects one by one points up something of the particular appeal that each may or may not have, it is the acts of choice and specialization which are important, for these both create anxiety and offer a way of dealing with it. The secondary school curriculum is largely organized around a series of choices which can be both intellectually and emotionally diminishing and because choice, specialization and examinations lead to anxiety, there is an unconscious curriculum which runs alongside the conscious one. The defence mechanisms of splitting, denial and projection are quite simply mapped out in secondary schools through the curriculum. This is because when children choose one set of subjects they give up others, and in so doing they symbolically give up parts of themselves. Even though the introduction of the national curriculum may have reduced the ease with which British children can give up learning subjects, examination choices are not compulsory. The crunch still comes with examinations, at GCSE and, more acutely, at 'A' levels. The improvement in getting girls to take science at GCSE is not followed through at 'A' levels which are far more critical in later career terms. What happens in any situation of anxiety is that feelings get split up and denied in order to cope. One expression of this 'coping' is simply to 'give up' mathematics, French, history, geography, or whatever is disliked or found too difficult.

This is because subjects function like persons, that is, they have to be related to and identified with, or not, as the case may be. One has to 'get on' with the subject. They can guide or obstruct one's progress through education and taking the 'wrong' subject can have a profound long-term effect, just like being in the 'wrong' relationship. Subjects, if they function as transitional objects, have to be reliable. After all, they are turned to at moments of anxiety and they must be trustworthy – they must not let you down. Once subjects become little more than excuses for examinations and 'doing well' is more important than whether they are enjoyed or intellectually stimulating, reliability becomes all-important.

Increasingly, subjects symbolize the self in educational terms. They are both part of the self and not part of the self. The choice of a subject invites pupils to compare and contrast and then identify with, or otherwise position themselves as inside one subject and outside another. They have to announce publicly whether they are going to be an 'Arts' or a 'Science' person and they have to put up with the social consequences which in some schools may mean being called a 'boffin' or a 'scabby scientist'. Anoraks and 'train spotter' epithets are the caricatures of the techno-weenies. And subjects acquire the characteristics of a frightening parent. For example, some of the fear and loathing with which subjects are approached stems from an equation with parents who (rightly or wrongly) are expected to be unrewarding, unforgiving and monolithic. Metaphorically, the 'familiar' origins of subjects are most obvious when we talk of the 'parent' discipline, but there is more than a hint of this when subjects are referred to as 'hard' or 'soft'. We know that pupils choose subjects according to who they think will teach them, despite being advised not to; often in the face of a series of strategies designed to conceal exactly that information from the pupils.

Essentially, subjects embody feelings, just as people elicit feelings. They can make you feel good or bad about yourself. Feeling 'at home' in a subject, being able to 'get into it' and use its conventions for one's own expressive purposes is akin to using a teddy bear, blanket or whatever as a tool for mental growth. In the case of the baby it is used to 'manage' separation and then fill the time actively; in the case of the subject it is the difference we probably all remember between the lessons in which we were engaged and interested and those where our minds were elsewhere, in a perpetual daydream, willing the time away.

Even if subjects are not actively hated, for most children the week ahead is a mixture of good days and bad days and it is rare for a child to like all school subjects equally. Indeed, we assume this when we ask children what are their 'favourite' or 'best' subjects. When we do this we encourage them to 'split' and to locate their bad experiences of school in a definite place. This roller-coaster of highs and lows gets more dramatic in secondary school and contrasts with primary schooling where teaching and learning was a much more integrated process, and usually quite happy. Paradoxically, although pupils are meant to be more mature in secondary schools, the way that the schools are organized positively encourages a regression to primitive defence mechanisms by splitting up the curriculum into subjects and stressing the importance of disciplinary boundaries. It is especially striking how the language of feelings changes at secondary school – and very swiftly. Within two weeks of starting secondary school my daughter, a good all-rounder in primary school, began to say that she hated maths, was no good at it and would not, or could not, tell the teacher that she did not understand. As pupils begin to feel strongly about subjects rather than teachers, they begin to act out these feelings and they describe subjects in terms of love and hate much more forcibly than they did feelings about their primary school teachers. In extreme cases the strength of feeling about different subjects leads to truancy, for much 'bunking off' is associated with lessons that are disliked, and truancy is much more of a problem in secondary schools than it is in primary schools.

The Shift from Primary to Secondary School and from
Person-Based Teaching to Subject-Based Teaching

When children are in primary school they have very little choice about the work that they do: there is virtually no differentiation by subject and children are based in one classroom, with one teacher, where they do most of their work. The curriculum is largely delivered through 'topics' and 'projects', with children taking home to their parents 'maps' and 'webs' to show how mathematics, science, history and English really do all fit in. Even with the national curriculum, which was partly aimed at increasing the amount of science and technology done in primary schools, this general approach has not changed fundamentally. What specialization does occur tends to be restricted to music, art and PE. The whole orientation of teaching is *person*-based and not *subject*-based. The secondary school curriculum is quite different. There are teachers for different subjects, children move around the school and, at least after the first or second year of secondary school, there is a choice of subject. In the primary school feelings towards learning and school in general are wrapped up with feelings about the particular teacher, whereas in the secondary school, although feelings about teachers are still important, they are progressively transferred onto subjects which gradually come to function as 'containers' in much the same ways as people can.

It is common for children to fear the transition to secondary school and to expect the school to be overwhelmingly large, full of bullies and strict, perverse or unfriendly teachers. Getting lost, being always in the wrong place and having to cart heavy bags around are regarded as almost inevitable. The only so called 'saving grace' is meant to be a wider choice of subjects and the chance to escape for some of the day from teachers and subjects that they dislike. These differences in organizational routine are nearly always viewed as simply practical arrangements, the costs and benefits of larger institutions. But their influence is far greater and they can have a profound effect on the way that identities are constructed, and gender identities in particular, which, in turn, can affect the polarization and gender stereotyping of subject choice.

As teaching moves away from being organized around a whole person and towards the more specialized and fragmented notion of the subject, these subjects are, at some level, required to substitute for the person (the teacher) in framing the pupils' sense of self. A couple of years on into secondary school and pupils are required to make crucial choices, prior to taking the GCSE examinations. Although, officially, it is conscious considerations such as future careers and entry to higher education which are meant to determine these choices, the milieu of anxiety which surrounds option choice time invites unconscious factors to play a major part. For the request to choose options is a form of enhancing or privileging one side of themselves at the expense of another, and is akin to identifying or dis-identifying with people who have been emotionally important. Schools, through their organizational and examining practices, invite pupils to define and situate themselves in terms of some notion of difference and otherness – and they ask pupils to do this at exactly the moment that teaching becomes most depersonalized, that is, when it becomes subject-based rather than person-based.

Looked at through the lens of object relations none of this is odd. The shift from one primary caretaker to another, or to several, echoes or replays the situation in infancy when the mother gives over her child to someone else, often the father, to share the care. In both instances the move provides a precondition for later growth. It allows both further internal differentiation and differentiation between the self and others. This is well understood in the psychoanalytical literature – fathers relate to children in ways that are fundamentally different from the way mothers relate to their children (Samuels, 1993) – but this sort of shift is also the basis of Durkheim's (1960) distinction between mechanical and organic solidarity (types of social structure). Offered as a way of explaining how societies evolve and grow more complex, it parallels the pattern of individual growth. Each type of solidarity implies a different form of connectedness. Mechanical solidarity meant relating to others on the basis of sameness and, at the psychic level, projection as a technique would work very well, there being little call to get to grips with difference: whereas under organic solidarity relationships the whole structure of society is based on difference and interdependence. Primary and secondary schools may be thought of in a similar way, with primary schools being mainly based on a form of mechanical solidarity and secondary ones on organic solidarity.

This may seem a bit abstract, but the rationale of large secondary schools is that they can offer variety and choice to pupils because staff can specialize. This practice is rarely questioned in mainstream education, although it stands in marked contrast to some alternative methods such as the Steiner system which stresses the need for continuity of teacher for the whole of a child's school career, at least until the relatively late age of 14, when some specialization is introduced. Being taught different subjects by different people clearly changes the meaning of learning. It introduces the idea of disciplines and boundaries, of competing paradigms, of choice and of escape.

When, as an undergraduate, I was given the definition of economics, 'What economists do', I felt short-changed. It was unsatisfactory and a poor excuse for failing the proper abstract task of definition. Without going into the nature of definitions I am much more willing now to accept it, because it plays down the idea of a subject as abstract and plays up the idea that a subject is a representation produced by real people. A subject is a social institution that consists of people as well as rhetoric, models, tools and techniques (McCloskey, 1986; Nelson *et al.*, 1987). I only want to add that what economists 'do' is a form of behaviour and as such is affected by economists' unconscious drives as much as by their conscious ones.

A friend of mine often says that economics is a form of madness built on splitting and denial: it operates by assuming rational action and profit-maximizing behaviour and by denying or eliminating all evidence to the contrary. In making this observation, this ex-economist is testifying to how much the subject meets or fails to meet a set of emotional needs. Maybe it is unfair to pick on economics and all subjects are a form of madness; certainly any subject, once institutionalized, acquires a culture or character which exists in the mind of individuals and affects the choices that they make. There is, after all, both a push and a pull at work. The content of a subject as well as its gendered culture can attract or deter according to how wrapped up in their own processes of gender formation individuals are. The next chapter looks further at how the different developmental trajectories of boys and girls fit into educational structures which are themselves also prone, through the principles of selection, to polarization.

Chapter 7

Polarization, Subjects and Choice: 'Male Wounds' and 'Crossroads'

Object Relations as a Theory of Subject Choice

The overall argument of the last chapter was that the move from primary to secondary school was profoundly disruptive socially and emotionally and the cause of much anxiety for many children and their parents. Despite a series of educational changes intended to increase parental choice, getting a child into a desired school, especially a secondary one, has become a highly fraught process. For the child, the transition to secondary school is both the focus of a number of frightening stories and a major, looming hurdle to be surmounted. It means learning a lot of new personal and organizational routines, getting-up times, routes to school, and having to carry heavy bags all day as pupils move from class to class and teacher to teacher. The rate of theft is high and lockers, where they exist, are easily damaged. For many children the bullying that they have heard about is a reality, even if it does not go so far as the knifings and bogwashes that the urban myths relate. All pupils are less firmly rooted in one place than they were in primary school and often feel distinctly displaced, lonely and disintegrated.

The purpose of this chapter is to show how object relations theory can explain the link between what happens during the transition from junior to secondary school and the polarization of subject choice and sex-stereotyping of subjects. It does this by exploring two accounts of gender development, each of which stress the particular crises which girls and boys or adolescents have to face, and it links them to the structural demands for polarization which seem to be inscribed in educational organizations and through which young people have to pass. More specifically, it accepts the challenge offered by John Pratt (1984) to identify the mechanism of polarization. As he observes, we may know the general direction of gender and subject choice, namely that boys prefer science and girls the arts, but we know nothing of the mechanisms which produce this pattern.

Yet it is polarization as much as stereotyping that needs to be understood. For polarization is progressive and systematic. It was a central theme in the sociology of education when access to educational opportunity was the major research paradigm and the overriding issue seemed to be how best to explain the interaction between class and education (Lacey, 1970), or how deviance could be an outcome of education (Hargreaves, 1967). More recently, these studies have been referred to collectively as differentiation–polarization or d–p theory (Hammersley, 1985; Shilling, 1991, 1992) and whilst this is not the place to add to the debate about how empirically well-founded this theory is, it is appropriate to note how pervasive polarization is as a feature of educational organizations and that gender divisions are highly likely to take the same general form for purely organizational/structural reasons. In relation to curriculum choice the important point is the *polarizing context* of education and the survival of the polarized subject choice, even after particular subjects have changed their gender and switched from being masculine to feminine or vice versa.

Subject choice, whether for GCSE, or 'A' level or degree course, is a fairly discrete event, as are the examinations which precede and follow it. But the shadow of anxiety or worry about whether the choices were the right ones can last for years. It becomes part of the general process of maintaining, negotiating and qualifying one's identity, whilst the most striking feature of subject choice is that the freer it is, the more gendered it is. The national curriculum simply delays the critical choices to the post-compulsory phase. In this context it may be wrong to think of subject choice as an individual choice at all, but a matter of individuals interpreting the cultural knowledge available to them and playing the game of life according to the known rules (Gambetta, 1987).

Whatever theory of polarization is brought to bear on these phenomena, it needs to operate both at the level of individual choice and that of culture – that is, of the gendering of subjects. The reason object-relations theory has a particular purchase here is that by being based on relationships it helps explain how and why subjects can be experienced, and manipulated, like people. As unconscious factors such as developmental stage and its characteristic crises affect how we relate to people, so too do they affect how we relate to subjects. This means that educational choices such as choosing, specializing and dropping a subject may bear less relation to rational or future-oriented factors (anticipated career, for example) and more to past feelings about parents, siblings, and teachers and the relationships with all these people that have become embodied in the subjects. At a

107

broader level, object relations suggests how the established cultures of subjects embody forms of defence against the predominant anxiety or anxieties that are inherent in their main tasks. When these tasks are presented to adolescents as choices they tend to be chosen or rejected on unconscious grounds.

Whilst no one consciously says 'Because I am a boy I will do physics' or 'Because I am a girl I will do French' something, nevertheless, sorts out the subjects by gender pretty efficiently, and the bi-polar pattern of boys taking science whilst girls follow arts courses gets deeper or more fixed at each successive stage of the educational ladder. Subjects or disciplines, of course, are strongly gendered parts of the educational landscape and if individual gender identity has been 'successfully' constructed we should not be surprised that by 16 or so girls choose the feminine subjects and boys the masculine ones. It would be naive to expect anything else, yet schools present subject choice as though it was gender-neutral and seem surprised when efforts to encourage pupils into gender-atypical choices fail. In part this is because of our poor understanding of the processes in play. We still know rather little of why more men than women choose physics or more women than men choose English, French or sociology. If it was all conditioning we would not see the situation that so often brings grief to teachers and parents when pupils who had previously succeeded in gender-atypical subjects make gender-stereotypic choices at the last, crucial, moment. Something seems to undermine good intentions and, at the most critical points, lead to more conventional choices.

A subsidiary purpose of this chapter is, therefore, to explain the return or reversion to gender-stereotypic subject choices and/or why subjects retain an appeal based on some aspect of gender despite all the efforts over the last decade or so, inside of schools and out, to break down these associations. It suggests that gendered and polarized subject choices cannot be explained purely in terms of their content or image, or even by the sexism of teachers, but by polarization which is both a cause and consequence of gender. Gender identities are formed around difference and anything in the environment that establishes, legitimizes or maintains difference is liable to be used opportunistically by the processes which make up gender relations.

Of course, being good at or interested in a subject and choosing it are different matters; both show strong signs of being affected by gender and in both cases unconscious determinants play a part. Over and above obvious things such as 'rigged' timetabling which make hybrid combinations of arts and science subjects impossible (though this is becoming less common) the factors affecting subject choice seem to draw their power as much from unconscious processes as from conscious ones. Although developmental studies seem to show that boys have an edge over girls when set tasks involving the manipulation of objects in three dimensions, on the whole, the evidence for explaining subject specialization by innate or cognitively-based sex differences is poor (Feingold, 1988; Hyde, 1990). Most of the explanations of the male/female science/arts split focus on the social character of subjects, their staffing and cultures and the practical and political details of timetabling and organizing the curriculum (Whyld, 1983; Kelly, 1981, 1987; Pratt *et al.*, 1984; Woods, 1990; Riddell, 1989; Goodson, 1993).

In liberal theory, choice is usually presented as good, and in most respects it probably is, but it is also often a moment of crisis which, by definition, is a moment of difficulty. Certainly, it appears that anxiety and distress levels rise for adolescents (Cairns *et al.*, 1991; McGee and Stanton, 1992; Ollendick *et al.*, 1994) even if not all of the rise can be attributed to impending examinations and subject or career choice. But choice can overwhelm with the enormity and the range of issues to be faced, and amongst the common responses are avoidance and/or reversion to tradition. In gender terms this often means 'choosing' stereotypical life-scripts. When situations become risky and/or more pressured, such as when options have to be chosen and subjects dropped, gender divisions become more marked. In particular, the subjects chosen are generally those which comfort. Hence the appeal that different subjects have for each sex relates both to the epistemological characteristics of the subjects and to the gradually more sex-differentiated responses of being put in pressured and anxiety-inducing situations. School organization and the pattern of emotional/psychological development thus converge around the demand that choices be made.

The Meaning of School Transfers and Subject Choice

The main difference between primary and secondary schools, after sheer size, is that teaching in primary schools is generally person-based, with one teacher taking children for most subjects; whilst secondary school teaching separates teachers and subjects. The last chapter explored some of the emotional meanings, both of the subjects themselves and the shift. It stressed that in the primary school attachment to work was directly mediated by attachment to the teacher and that, on the whole, much concern was given to maintaining good relations with pupils. By contrast, teaching in secondary schools is organized by subject and the attachment of children to teachers is mediated by 'subject' rather than by a person. Dislike of the teacher turns easily into dislike of the subject and levels of alienation rise – a fact which systems of year tutors and pastoral care are meant to compensate for.

The shift from primary to secondary school signals to children a shift in their identifications. It starts with choosing the secondary school (at least theoretically) and, according to the choice, some friends are kept and others lost. It is followed, a little later, with a choice of subjects. Schools, parents and pupils monitor which subjects they like, or do well in, and gradually they are invited to identify with subjects, that is, with something more abstract than a person. As they progress through school and take successive mock and real examinations they are obliged to choose some subjects and drop others. Some subjects are obviously dropped with relief, others with regret. Schools tend to stress how important option choices are: they tell pupils what a difference they will make to their futures and that hard choices have to be made. The whole act of choice is surrounded with a great sense of pressure. While schools counsel children not to choose subjects on the basis of who is going to teach them, and may even withhold that crucial piece of information, it is clear that this is exactly what pupils do if they can. Liking and fear, both conscious and unconscious, affect both pupils and perceptions of progress. Parents often think that their child might have done better with a different teacher or, conversely, wish that they or their child could please the teacher. Recently an 'A' level student told me that although he had got reasonably good grades and was assured of a place on the degree course he wanted, he was disappointed that his lowest grade, a C, was in the subject that had been taught by the teacher he liked best. He had wanted to do well for that teacher. Just as important, though possibly less obvious, is the way that subjects start to become the basis of discrimination between pupils. The processes are complex and what may seem like self-selection as in 'I am not good enough to keep on with physics, Latin, chemistry, etc.' may, in fact, be engineered by the system. In many schools, particularly before the introduction of the national curriculum, a covert form of streaming was signalled by whether or not a child took French. Even now, with the national curriculum, less able students are channelled into domestic science and business studies and perceived levels of ability are easily read off from the package of subjects a pupil takes. The most aggressive form of subjects choosing who should take them, however, is gender. Whenever we refer to subjects as being more or less 'girl-friendly' or 'boy-friendly' we acknowledge that subjects have cultures which can be enticing or off-putting. Just as with teachers, there are some subjects that pupils can identify with and some that they cannot – and a key part of this process is how gendered those subjects are felt to be.

Gender and Polarization

There are dozens of reason why subjects are treated differently, many of which have nothing in particular to do with gender, though they may serve to reinforce gender divisions. Theoretically, the issue is often presented as one of priority i.e. which divisions come first – class, gender or race? Whilst this has been a major theme in feminist thought, no final answer is possible as feminism evolves in relation to the practical, political situations it seeks to analyse and transform. Which divisions are more entrenched and powerful varies according to time, place and opportunism. However, because sexual divisions allow little scope for intermediate positions, gender often takes a polarized form in the way that class and ethnic divisions may not. But there are other reasons why the issue of gender and polarization raises the question of priority. As a process, polarization can be seen either as rooted in the individual, an outgrowth of the individual defence mechanism of splitting writ large, or in the society. To survive in societies built around fissure individuals have to place themselves in opposing camps, from within which a greater degree of variation may be permitted.

In the 1980s, attempts were made to intervene and reverse polarization by making science and technology more 'girl-friendly' through programmes such as GIST (Girls into Science and Engineering) and WISE (Women in Science and Engineering) and through TVEI (Technical and Vocational Education Initiative) which used contract compliance principles to ensure that sex discrimination was avoided (at least overtly). At the same time, many feminist scholars argued that girls were not underachieving, especially not in mathematics (Burton, 1988, 1990; Walkerdine and Walden, 1985; Walkerdine, 1990; Kenway and Willis, 1990). But discussion rarely got beyond matters of presentation, marketing and the stereotyping of girls' abilities. More fundamentally, because studies tended to be subject-specific, that is, they concentrated on physics, mathematics, or languages, the explanations were slightly different in each instance. Unless polarization itself was focused on, as Pratt acknowledged, it was very easy to end up with different explanations of what turned boys off languages or girls off physics, and no explanation at all of why or how subjects could change their gender over time. The most popular, social constructionist, accounts of gender were fine at making a dislike of science or language work perfectly plausible, once the subjects had acquired a gendered character, but they could not explain why they became gendered in the first place. For this, more historical/political analyses are necessary (Riddell, 1992), and these very often reveal unexpected consequences, such as the hold that classics had over educational ideas in the nineteenth century, de-legitimizing science first for boys but then, in an even more devastating way for girls, as the pioneers of girls' education over-conformed to the model set by boys' schools (Phillips, 1990).

Subject choices are never just about subjects. Much more comes into play. Most schools limit subject choice by demanding that combinations are chosen from within 'blocks', but even where there is a so-called 'free choice', factors such as the teacher or what subjects friends are likely to choose matter considerably. Also, whether the school is single-sex or mixed makes an enormous difference. One of the most surprising of all official education reports was the 1975 HMI's *Report on the Curriculum in Secondary Schools* which revealed that sex-stereotyping of subjects and polarization of choice was greater in coeducational schools than in the single-sex schools, even the inexpertly staffed and poorly equipped single-sex girls' schools. More girls took science subjects in these schools than they did in the better equipped and better staffed coeducational schools. The importance of this report was that it showed that something other than laboratories and qualifications made the difference.

At the time that it was published the report punctured a general complacency about mixed schooling as progressive and led, briefly, to some interest in single-sex schooling, though not to any reversal of its general decline. Fifteen or so years later, when newspapers as well as the government began a series of surveys, single-sex girls' schools consistently showed a marked superiority in academic performance over all other types of school. The first of these surveys, by the *Financial Times* (March 1992), was especially interesting because it only surveyed private schools and showed that it was the single-sex day schools, not the ancient, high-status boarding schools for boys that did best, with the coeducational schools trailing a long way behind. Until then, the whole single-sex/coeducational picture had been muddied by the problem of sorting out class effects from the effects of different sorts of school. When the debate was focused mainly on the state schools and the majority of single-sex schools were private and/or selective, it was difficult to know how much of the superior academic performance of children educated in single-sex schools should be attributed to selection, social class or the milieu of gender relations. These difficulties have not disappeared and interpreting the results will always be contentious, but there is now enough evidence to suggest an independent interactional effect is at work which affects academic performance.

After all, a mixed class *is* different to a single-sex one, though a denial of this is an odd but fundamental part of 'progressive' pedagogy. Being with, or away from, friends feels different and affects the learning experience. And friendship groups for the majority of schoolchildren are single-sex, even in mixed schools. Wanting to stay with friends or avoid being the 'odd one out' is rational if it reduces the chances of harassment, but it is also a function of unconscious identification with other pupils and with the subject itself. But there is a further link between the emotional and unconscious meanings of 'subjects' and their role in reproducing gender identities which is, once more, tied up with anxiety.

The 'Good' Breast and the 'Bad' Subject: The Psychological Bases of Splitting

For both sexes the move from primary to secondary school and the externally imposed demand to choose some subjects over others mimics, or repeats in a symbolic form, the initial separation from the mother (or other primary caretaker). When we choose subjects we are obliged to redefine ourselves and make a public statement about what sort of person we are, or hope to be. It is, perhaps, the first significant choice of identity. As we select subjects we select to drop some people, friendships and teachers who have become parts of ourselves. In this process something personal always gets lost and the parallels are not lost on the unconscious, however dimly they are sensed. Because of the human capacity to remember and what Freud called the compulsion to repeat responses to past traumas, human action is affected by the individual's past. In this case the memory of loss and the adjustments made to it form a repertoire of action which are called upon time and time again in later life. Formulaic solutions based on infancy become the bases of choices made in adolescence and later. When those choices come at a particularly fraught time, for example at the height of adolescence, which is exactly when some of the most critical educational decisions are made, they are even more likely to be made along lines which correspond most to unconscious needs. At this stage, anxiety is multiple and multiplied and the 'old' solutions such as splitting and projective identification are the easiest to hand.

The assumption underlying all psychoanalytical theory is that it is difficult for humans to reconcile opposing and conflicting feelings and that one of the strategies for dealing with this problem is found by splitting. In the Kleinian version the infant is described as experiencing the world as chaotic and unpredictable, with sensations of pleasure and comfort succeeding each other apparently randomly. Producing these erratic states is a breast which is 'good' when it is there doing its job of providing milk and 'bad' when it is absent. For the infant the world effectively consists of an alternation between this 'good' breast and the 'bad' breast. Even later, when a connection between the two 'breasts' is made, the realization is so uncomfortable that the infant and the infant in all of us often reverts to a simpler, more dichotomous view of the world.

This splitting is thus a defence against terror and anxiety, whether that anxiety is induced by a mother's 'failure' to be exactly what the infant wants or by a school announcing that the time to choose options or fill in UCAS forms has come around again. In infancy, the problem is how to manage ambivalence or contain conflicting good or bad feelings about the same person, and an early solution is often found in a combination of projection (to project is to export awkward, uncomfortable feelings and treat them as if they belonged to another person, which is psychologically easier than to own them) and splitting.

Though infancy and adolescence are not the same, they share similar survival strategies. All childrearing creates internal fissure and dislocations with inevitable episodes of disappointment or frustration which create, in turn, the need and opportunity for devising strategies of coping with them. As a result, all children are left with ambivalences towards their parents. A common way of dealing with the parental failure to immediately and exactly provide what a baby desires is to endow/invent another object with some of the same comforting and pleasure-giving capacity: a displacement into some symbolic activity. This, according to Winnicott, is the basis of survival, creativity and symbol formation. In chapter 6, while I argued that academic subjects can function as transitional objects (as a type of symbol), I did not point out that transitional objects need not always be benign. Yet, for the notion of transitional object to be helpful it must include disliked objects as well as liked ones where creativity does not flourish (Richards, 1994).

At the time that he wrote, Winnicott's formulations of early psychic life made an impact partly because they departed from the prevailing and somewhat gloomy ideas associated with Melanie Klein and her rather oddly named 'depressive position'. This referred to the moment when the infant realizes that good and bad experiences might have the same source. Although this integration is an achievement, it is difficult to hold on to and the possibility/threat of disintegration, or of reversion to a view of the world as dichotomous and where good and bad experiences are external, is ever-present. At the heart of the difference between Klein and Winnicott is a view of how much difference the environment can make to the course of an individual's development. Klein is rather more pessimistic than Winnicott, who saw emotional growth not purely as a matter of inner conflicts and their resolution, but of how the infant adapted to the environment and how that environment adapted to the infant. Yet, despite their different emphases, both Klein's and Winnicott's approaches illuminate the process of gender and subject specialization. The fact that some subjects, mathematics perhaps most publicly, are feared and others enjoyed parallels the 'good' and the 'bad' breast that Klein suggests is part of all early life.

It is fairly easy to translate these ideas into social terms and see how social structures like schools are an environment: demanding choice and providing the preconditions for polarization or splitting. In such a context it is also fairly easy to see how good and bad subjects/disciplines resonate with early experiences of the good and bad breast. The consequences of an unconscious equation of academic subject with self and with pleasure or pain and the 'solution' of splitting is reinforced by a teaching pattern which ceases to have one teacher taking pupils for most, if not all, subjects and moves over to one where subjects and teachers are 'cut up' or bounded. Together, the organizational basis of teaching and an increased dose of anxiety form the basis for a sex-stereotyped and polarized pattern of subject choice. Added to all this are the specific and somewhat different developmental paths taken by each sex.

Anxiety and Subject Choice: Men, 'Male Wounds' and 'Dis-identification'

Fear and anxiety as driving or motivating forces appear in many psycho-analytical accounts of gender identity, both male and female. For example, Rosalind Coward (1992) locates anxiety at the very heart of female identity, as the expression of a deep set of problems and contradictions and the search for impossible goals or objects. Lyn Brown and Carol Gilligan (1992) identify a crossroads which girls are obliged to traverse in adolescence and at which, under the impact of an inescapable and internalized demand for perfection, they exchange self-assurance and knowledge for insecurity. Nancy Chodorow's (1978) analysis of the long-term consequences of mothering in the western world turns on a view of what happens to boys and men when they are prematurely separated from their mothers, has been used to explain many aspects of adult behaviour, including subject choice (Harding and Sutoris, 1987). However, it is the work of psychologist Liam Hudson in a series of books (Hudson, 1966, 1972, 1982) and, more recently, with his wife (Hudson and Jacot, 1991) that delves deepest into the nature of male intellectual life.

Their argument about the 'male wound' does not differ very substantially from Chodorow, though it acknowledges Greenson (1968) as the more original. Boys are required to separate more fundamentally from their mothers than are girls, that is, they have to 'dis-identify' and are set the essentially abstract task of identifying with their often absent fathers or with some aspect of their fathers' role. This process leads, characteristically, to a confusion of 'things with people' and 'people as things' and the more 'male' the man the deeper the 'wound', although there are many patterns and variants on the forms of intimacy or identification a child of either sex might have with each of their parents. There are both costs and benefits associated with this male wound. Men are likely to be more driven than women and they appear to have more energy. This drive is rooted in a desire to regain an intimacy with women that girls have not lost in the first place and it is this drive that accounts for the obsessive and 'passionate' qualities of their work. The desire to be re-united is the hidden source both of intellectual passion and of men's greater profligacy or promiscuity.

Thus, Hudson and Jacot go further than either Winnicott or Chodorow in their discussion of the 'male wound' for they argue that this is exactly what drives men on. The wound has a capacity to engender fascination with the impersonal and, they write, 'such passions will be the more enduringly gratifying the more completely divorced they are from human relationships'. This capacity for passionate absorption and abstraction is more characteristic of men than women and has been advantageous in evolutionary terms. For Hudson and Jacot, it is one of life's paradoxes that the tendency to confuse people with things and vice versa should be of such benefit.

They illustrate their thesis of imaginative energy being rooted in the male wound with episodes from the lives of Newton, Freud and Skinner and with a phase in the history of the Institute of Advanced Thought at Princeton. In the case of B.F. Skinner, who invented a childrearing box in response to disgust with his daughter's nappies, they suggest that in Skinner's psychic world the fear of faeces was graphically contained by the box, which also provided a barrier between Skinner and his daughter. Perhaps even more fascinating is some of their unpublished data relating academic field to the conduct of personal relations which, they claim, consistently reveals celibate classical scholars, womanizing poets, much divorced but innovative biologists and sexist engineers. Typically, the male mind is preoccupied with formal models (including scientific method), with *idées fixes* and with violence (symbolic and real) and with psychological manoeuvres or personal feuds.

None of this, of course, is an area in which 'hard' evidence exists, but many of the examples they choose have clearly occurred to others. Anthony Storr (1988), in a study of the preconditions for creativity, mentions Isaac Newton, Winston Churchill and the once imprisoned civil servant Anthony Grey as having in common childhoods in which their mothers were either distant or absent. In each case their adaptation to this had led to great creativity in later life.

The male, essentially, has two choices for relating the personal to the impersonal: segregation or integration. If he chooses the former he is likely to choose science and use the impersonal to subjugate the personal. If he opts for integration, he is more likely to become an artist and struggle to recreate his initial union in symbolic terms. In general, 'scientific pursuits are associated with individuals who feel detached from the world' and 'value in science the opportunities it presents for controlling the world (i.e. orderly arrangement and meticulous accuracy or models)'. Hudson and Jacot claim that

> the possession of scientific 'knowledge' or 'fact' is an admirable substitute for a boy suffering separation anxiety. It can be depended upon, it cannot be denied or destroyed and it establishes order in an incomprehensible universe. In this manner scientific facts contribute to the male's sense of security by enriching his sense of self by 'possessing' knowledge.

The other side of this process produces artistic rather than scientific work, for the projects of art and science are in some ways similar. Both demand a reconciliation of intuitive judgment with technical control, both demand experiment, both can be fuelled by the fantasy of control and both reflect the need to treat the personal as though it were impersonal, that is, people as though they were things. When discussing the male artist, Hudson and Jacot argue that two propensities interact. The impulse that, for example, may become an obsessing preoccupation with pure form for an artist may lead to fetishism in another man. It is a delicate balance. Whilst the general argument of Hudson and Jacot, of Harding and Sutoris and, by implication, of Winnicott, is that science and technology offer safety and certainty and protection from the threat of disorder, in their final two chapters on artists and their muses Hudson and Jacot suggest that in the arts the male imagination can turn from its natural home in science and technology to the female body from which it originally took flight.

As these two authors are not interested in how women think, it is necessary to look elsewhere for a parallel account of girls' intellectual and gender development which might illuminate their typical subject choices. The gender and education paradox has always been that, as a whole, girls do very well in terms of examination passes and grades, rather better than boys until mid-adolescence – such that they cannot be honestly described as 'underachieving'. Thus, if a case is to be made about education as failing girls it has to be that, as a currency, educational qualifications have less exchange value for girls than boys and that their subject choices somehow let them down.

Maybe an absence of passion is the key and, to some extent, there is a hint of this type of explanation in the object relations accounts of Nancy Chodorow (1978), Lyn Mikel Brown and Carol Gilligan (1992). If the 'dis-identification' or 'male wound' theories rest on a view of boys as suffering a lifelong legacy of anxiety from a premature separation from their mother, which is channelled into a general preference for the more cut and dried subject areas such as mathematics and natural sciences, girls' subject choice is explained in terms of their protracted symbiosis or identification with their mothers. This mergedness and, indeed, difficulty with separation is what inclines them towards subjects which elevate and celebrate a capacity for empathy, sympathy and intuition, i.e. the arts, languages, humanities and the 'soft' social sciences. For girls, anxiety is resolved by closer identification, though this also leads them into the highly destructive 'perfect girl' syndrome just at the moment when they need to be able to hang on to a sense of trust in their own knowledge and capacity to learn from experience.

A striking and common feature of adolescent girls is an apparent inability to see a link between a future career and the subjects that they currently take (Weinreich-Haste, 1981; Furlong, 1986; Chisholm and Holland, 1986). Indeed, it is almost as if there is a perverse disjunction. This is generally explained either in terms of poor careers guidance or the de-railing effect of anticipating marriage and motherhood. However, the reason why girls fail to see career potential in the subjects that they follow may be connected to a more fundamental re-orientation, or rather disorientation, that goes on in adolescence. In a series of papers culminating in a book co-authored with Lynne Mikel Brown, Carol Gilligan has explored why young teenage girls appear to lose the feisty, self confidence and directness of their middle childhood years and replace it with a self deprecating, assumed and false ignorance. They fear being outspoken lest the knowledge that they have of relationships, themselves and other people, which comes from their experience to date, wrecks the idealised relationships that they are beginning to want above all.

Adolescent girls begin to be dominated by a standard of female perfection which does not come out of their experience but calls into question the reality that they have so far lived by. Brown and Gilligan (1992) argue that this image of perfection is closely tied to the idea of loss and is an idealization that replaces actual relationships with all their real difficulties. Swept up in this ideal image girls lose confidence in or deny what they really know, including the evidence of their own bodies, and become disconnected. The consequences of this range from the erratic, perverse and traditional educational decisions made by girls to the lifelong higher rates of depression suffered by women. There is quite a wide range of data from other sources which confirms this interpretation, not least the findings of the attribution theorist Kay Deaux (1977) who showed how assumptions about the reliability or unreliability of factors producing academic success or failure were incorporated by girls and boys into explanations of their own results in quite opposite ways. Whereas boys chose typically reliable factors such as intelligence to explain their success, and unreliable ones such as bad luck to explain failure, girls did the reverse. They interpreted good academic results as 'flukes', the result of unstable factors, and poor ones as evidence that they were not clever enough. On the basis of Brown and Gilligan's later work this is exactly what might have been predicted, at least for the girls.

Polarization as a Social Defence

The arts/science division is recognized as a background factor in a range of gender divisions, particularly in relation to occupations, but its role in keeping Britain an essentially masculine society is more rarely documented. This is because culturalist explanations tend to stop short of exploring exactly what it is about culture that produces deeper or shallower gender divisions, though they may describe and document the directions such divisions take and how they are perpetuated. We might expect that in a fiercely gendered culture boys and girls will take different subjects, but not that it is the sharp divisions rather than the traditional association of any particular subject with a gender that is critical. Yet it is the narrow 'A' level syllabus that makes for a polarization in subject choice and the narrowness that is tied to the divisiveness of British society. Exactly how this happens may seem arbitrary but, because timetables, university admissions policies, advisers and tradition deem hybrid combinations unwise for the seriously ambitious, and because so much depends on 'A' level results, more primitive and un-thought-out principles emerge to affect choices, particularly those regarded as especially critical.

Since the beginning of the 1990s there has been a stream of reports documenting the increasing social divisions of contemporary British society. Most of these relate to income and wealth which is now as unequal as it has been in the last hundred years. Mostly written from a social policy perspective they also confirm a common observation, namely that division and fissure or polarization are fundamental structural features of British society. One of the prime indicators used by one of these observers (Hofstede, 1980) is the degree of segregation between the sexes in schools and between subjects in higher education. And, indeed, gendered subject choice is more pronounced in Britain than in other equally highly educated societies, and more so in higher than in secondary education (Thomas, 1990). Thus division or polarization is a basic structural feature: as such it is a cause as much as a consequence of gender.

Although the association of gender with any particular subject varies cross-culturally, and not all countries show the marked divisions that occur in Britain, we should not be surprised to find that in Britain an unusually narrow 'A' level syllabus, a pronounced subject polarization by gender and a 'masculine' culture go together. Yet the depth and nature of gender divisions in education have not been widely understood or recognized as a cause of the 'decline' of science, nor have the unconscious factors which affect subject choice been given much credence. Yet both factors have a large part to play, especially in an education system such as the one in England and Wales which retains an unusually narrow curriculum for its most crucial set of examinations, the 'A' levels, *and* has depended for its increase in overall student numbers on improved participation rates by girls and women.

Conclusion

Polarization is both an organizing principle and a process of interpersonal interaction and comparison. It is evident in both formal structures and informal encounters. This chapter has concentrated on one example, subject choice, and attempted to explain its persistence in terms of a convergence between gender-typical developmental scenarios and organizational/ educational pressures which increase doses of anxiety. The next chapter looks at 'spontaneous' polarization between the sexes within school, whilst the penultimate chapter considers a particular polarization discourse – one which centres on single-sex or co-educational schooling.

Chapter 8

Classroom Interaction, Gender and Basic Assumptions

When children are very young, in nursery and kindergarten classes, boys and girls play together and invite each other to their birthday parties. This tends to last until about the end of the first term of primary school: thereafter having a girl to a boy's birthday party or vice versa becomes exceptional and the cause of much comment. Parents often regret the passing of this stage and wistfully remember when their children innocently played across sex boundaries. This voluntary sex-segregation gets more pronounced as children grow older and pass through the school system. Friendship groups are largely single-sex by the end of primary schooling and remain so throughout the secondary school years until, in adolescence, individual cross-sex friendships become viable once more. At this point individual attachments with a different, romantic or sexual basis are made and group dynamics recede in importance. The question is why does this occur? Why is there a largely voluntary process of single-sex grouping? Schools, after all, have become rather sensitive to the issue and avoid practices such as dividing the register into boys' names and girls' names or lining the sexes up separately.

Most explanations of this tend to be individualistic. Often they are based on seeing each sex as caught up in managing identities which would be compromised if they too obviously showed an interest in the opposite sex, so they strategically retreat into single-sex groupings in order to cope with the texture of social life in schools. Many of the explanations are plausible, coherent, even rational in the face of taunts, rough play, disruption and so on, and they nearly all see the emergence and deepening of sexual divisions as the product of individual responses to the situation rather than as a group phenomenon itself, even though many recognize that peer pressure and social control are at the heart of the matter.

122

Raphaela Best (1983) argues that boys are subject to what she calls the third curriculum, one that demands that they be tough, macho and hard. Whilst under this demand, contact with or interest in girls threatens to undermine their often vulnerable and embryonic sense of masculinity. And if they do not like the obviously boyish sports such as football, they are doubly under pressure not to befriend girls which, if they do, increases their chances of being called 'cissy' or 'sad'. Girls, too, are under pressure not to consort with boys. For them, emerging sexuality renders them both vulnerable and subject to new forms of social control. Sue Lees' (1986) focus on the tightrope that sexuality represents for pubertal girls is succinctly summarized as a no-win choice – if they are openly interested in sex they risk being called 'slags' whilst if they are not, they are defined as 'drags'. Heterosexual codes and patriarchal power limit and construct girls and women, whilst they enhance the power available to boys. Safety demands that girls increasingly restrict themselves to friendship with children of the same sex – preferably in a group setting if they are to avoid being labelled gay or 'lezzie' – whilst, if they are genuinely interested in a boy, girls' same-sex friendship groups provide an essential and necessary support to enable forays into the world of heterosexual relationships (Griffiths, 1992).

From the perspective of school organization the reasons not to make friendships with the opposite sex gradually accumulate. Covert ability groupings in formally mixed-ability classes are often single-sex de facto. Boys are often more disruptive than girls, or at least are perceived as such, and teachers bend with the wind, giving up any pretence at getting mixed-sex groups to work together (Tann, 1981). As GCSE looms, girls and boys tend to make sex-stereotyped subject choices which further segregate the sexes. Moreover, as boys increasingly dominate the culture of the school, both physically and in terms of the male discourses that they can call upon (Walkerdine, 1981; Walker, 1988), a significant minority behave in ways that are very close to sexual harassment (Mahony, 1985; Herbert, 1989). Female teachers and female pupils respond to this somewhat differently, with female pupils tending to keep their heads down, determined to avoid provocation and work hard (Stanley, 1986) whilst teachers, having responsibility for the whole class, give boys more time, attention and teacher talk, even though this may be the very last thing that they wish to do (Spender, 1980; French and French, 1984; LaFrance, 1991).

In none of these accounts are group processes primary and there is hardly any sense of a push towards group formation which exploits sexual divisions. In other areas of social science it is commonplace to view one institution, say capitalist employers, as exploiting another, say the sexual division of labour, to pay lower wages to women than men, but this analysis is rarely translated into the educational context. As David Hargreaves (1990) argues, the bulk of educational thought is deeply individualistic. Yet polarized, single-sex groupings may be seen from a group perspective. Institutions have to format themselves, they need to establish sub-groups to survive and function, and gender divisions facilitate this process. There is an ideological reason for this, which is that sex-polarized groups exaggerate and enhance the identity of each other thereby increasing the chances of heterosexual unions. If schools need to make groups, they also need some form of internal structure. Although this line of argument sails close to the winds of functionalism, the main point is that sex-based polarization cannot always be reduced to individual processes or needs. Groups have their own dynamics.

In this context psychoanalysis might be thought inappropriate as it is frequently criticized for being overly individualistic. A common charge is that it fails to take account the social, economic or cultural settings in which individuals live and concentrates, instead, on the inner world. Nevertheless, the work of Wilfrid Bion (1961) on group dynamics and the different levels at which groups operate has been extremely influential. Though relatively unexplored in the educational context, its potential for understanding how groups in schools help consolidate gender differences is considerable.

Bion's Basic Assumptions

In chapter 1 I mentioned a Freudian account (Holmes, 1967) of one sort of educational group, the university seminar, where individual members were bonded together symbolically by rituals and routines which re-enacted a form of patricide and resurrection. The routine destruction and reaffirmation were analysed as necessary stages for the intellectual development of the group and protection from devastation either by guilt or fear. A similar sort of exercise is possible using Bion's typology of the three basic and unconscious assumptions ('fight/flight', 'dependency' and 'pairing') which, he argues, drives and dominates much group behaviour.

Work rehabilitating soldiers at the end of the Second World War led Bion to think radically about the nature of group process with the result that he arrested the individualism of psychoanalytical thought and revived Freud's early interest in group psychology. He is best remembered for stressing that, in addition to the obvious, overt tasks that justify a group's existence, there was another, unconscious, level at which groups also operated. He demonstrated that groups have, or soon develop, a collective interest in their own survival which may often outlive their original purpose. The practices which serve this survival interest often cut across and undermine the ostensible task of the group and form the 'basic assumption' of the group. An easy example of this can be seen in the difficulty most organizations have with ending meetings on time. Whatever punctuality norm governs the start of meetings it is much harder to end on time, just as saying goodbye at a station or after a dinner party can be painfully protracted. The very people who want to get away find that they cannot and, indeed, themselves behave in ways which prolong or continue the meeting, the farewells or whatever. Individuals may think that there is someone else using the group for their own purposes, when it is really the group using the individuals. What is happening in this sort of situation is that the group is asserting its right to continue over the desire of the individuals to leave, or over the overt task of the group – the business meeting or social event.

Concentrating, then, on the unconscious, group-based dynamic, Bion noted that groups produced both a mentality and culture (or feel) which had to be negotiated as much as the other members of the group had to be negotiated. The group mentality was a unanimous expression of the will of the group and it made individuals feel distinctly uncomfortable if they stepped out of line. The group culture was a function of the conflict between the individual's desires and the group mentality and, together, the mentality and the culture amounted to what Bion termed the basic assumption of the group. This was entirely a group property: individuals contributed to it unconsciously, often in spite of themselves, and it took one of three basic forms, 'dependency', 'fight/flight' and 'pairing'. Whichever form was dominant (and this would shift around) individual members of the group would find it very hard to circumvent or act independently.

The need for survival caught up all the members of the group, either in a pattern of fighting or running away, in a preoccupation with a leader and how well he or she did their job, or in an interest in a couple, that is, two group members who had differentiated themselves from the rest of the group and who were treated as a sexual, reproductive couple. Although, as Samuels (1993) points out, Bion gives no explanation of why there are three and only three basic assumptions, and certainly Bion makes no reference to gender divisions per se within groups, the framework is a fertile one which handles many of the observations reported about informal group behaviour, including those that run along gender lines. All three basic assumption groups may be seen to play a part in the groupings which formally and informally characterize school life (the main teacher/pupil relationship is essentially a group based on dependency principles) but it is the 'pairing' basic assumption group that plays a key part in the formation of single-sex groupings.

A rather obvious way of viewing the increasingly antagonistic nature of gender relations in schools is to see them as examples of groups in the grip of fight/flight group relations, whereas groups which form around 'queen bee' children are groups oscillating between a pairing and a dependency function, especially when there is much competition for the status of being the 'best friend' or lieutenant of the most favoured child. Many children's groups seem to have as their basic *raison d'être* the exclusion of certain other children and these may be seen as examples of groups in the grip of a fight/flight basic assumption. Dependency, as a basic assumption, clearly runs through much group life in schools. Teachers and pupils are engaged most of the time in struggling around it, with teachers sometimes wishing to assert their leadership and sometimes trying to relinquish it in order to make the pupils work on their own. From the pupils' perspective, some of the time they try to usurp the teacher, whilst at other moments they apply themselves to making the teacher responsible for everything, including their learning. Fight/flight tactics are also evident in many school groupings, both in the playground and in the classroom, where real fights and flights take place. The overt support for competition that schools give, especially in sports, is a form of a fight/flight basic assumption group in operation, as is the group-based hysteria associated with examinations. However, it is the 'pairing' basic assumption that most affects the gender divisions within the group. Similarly, though it works in the opposite direction, a group might energetically and collectively attempt to prevent pairing by ridiculing anyone who looks like attempting it.

When a group is in the grip of a 'pairing' basic assumption it jumps to the conclusion that a sexual, reproductive relationship is about to occur or is occurring between two individuals (they may be two individuals of the same sex – this does not matter). The behaviour of the rest of the group becomes oriented towards this special relationship which is fantasized about, feared, supported, encouraged, denied, sabotaged, etc. An example of how different basic assumptions drive societies or, rather, how groups override individuals is provided by Lewis Coser's (1974) description of 'greedy institutions'. To illustrate his thesis about the lengths to which greedy institutions can go he cites the superficially discrepant attitudes towards marriage and sexuality of the theologically very different Jesuits and Mormons. Under conditions of external threat (the early days of the Mormon community in Salt Lake City and the inherently hostile situation encountered by any missionary order) the two religious communities evolved different solutions to the same problem

– namely, how to maintain full commitment to the group from all its members. In both cases, individuals forming couples and withdrawing into themselves and private, dyadic relationships were understood as the major threat. The Jesuits' solution was to impose a rule of celibacy and the Mormons' to impose a rule of polygamy: opposite strategies, but the same problem. For the group to survive, the pairing of individuals into couples had to be prevented. For these communities salvation through pairing was not available or was inappropriate; the fight/flight assumption was more powerful and it won out. Group coherence was maintained, the enemy remained without rather than within and the groups survived without recourse to a manufactured internal enemy as happened in the witch-hunting communities of New England (Erikson, 1966).

Single-sex school friendship groups can be seen in the same light. Children pairing off threatens the group, and groups of children take strong decisive action to prevent it. They make fun of any incipient romantic attachment. Being accused of loving or even liking a child of the opposite sex is, for many children, one of the most hurtful charges than can be levelled at them. They feel utterly defenceless when so branded and are unable to refute the charge or retaliate. What is happening is that while the group may be moving into a 'pairing' basic assumption mode it is currently stuck in a 'fight/flight' mode: either way pairing is clearly a group issue. If a particular child has a real interest in friendship with another of the opposite sex it has to be kept to out-of-school time and out of the group, for contact within school is exceedingly dangerous. Whatever happens, the group is more important than the individual and it produces behaviour from individuals to combat threats to the group. Thus, for example, if individuals look like pairing off, sanctions against such deviants are brought into play. When a child is excluded, bullied, teased or taunted with liking a particular boy or girl it will effectively stop them doing it, for it is group behaviour that rules and if they act 'responsibly' themselves they risk losing their own place in the group.

However, children grow and change, groups shift around, overt tasks change and single-sex groups persist because the pairing assumption becomes stronger and more of a justification for the group. As children get older, group survival becomes explicitly based on pairing. One ethnographic study of girls' friendship groups found that a good part of their activities focused around supporting individual girls in their attempts to establish heterosexual relationships (Griffiths, 1995). Encouragement, planning, sympathy, censure and advice, and a 'home' to return to were provided, placing the single-sex groups not in opposition to heterosexual unions but as a means of moving towards them. In this way, the single-sex girls' groups perpetuate the basic assumption group mentality of pairing. In the context of the school as a whole, group the polarization of intermediate single-sex groups functions to maintain and promote the ideology of heterosexuality. The belief in coeducation is essentially an 'innocent' one; it assumes that contact between the sexes can and should be asexual and without conflict. Even when coeducation is promoted as aiding heterosexual relations, the vision is of harmonious heterosexual relations. When voluntary, informal separation takes the place of formal segregation within coeducational schools it may indeed be performing the same function, but through sex-segregation, not without it.

Conclusion

This chapter has scraped the surface of seeing gender divisions as a group phenomenon, of applying Bion's basic assumption groups to the gendered polarization of informal groups in schools and to the idea that conflict and cooperation might both be integral to gender relations as a number or writers have suggested (Scanzoni, 1972; Sen, 1992). It is quite possible that the subject polarization that is deeper in the coeducational than the single-sex school is a function of the 'fight/flight' syndrome as much as the 'pairing' one. To repeat, we choose against subjects as much as for them and this can be another expression of fight/flight, especially when subject choice becomes a group phenomenon. To go further with any of these ideas requires empirical research but, minimally, this chapter has tried to suggest reasons why and how gender is a group phenomenon, why gender divisions recur and what broader functions they serve.

Chapter 9

Fears, Fantasies and Division in Single-Sex Schools

Anxiety and fantasy do not only affect behaviour in schools, they affect how educational issues are debated. Some topics are much harder than others to discuss rationally and of these the merits and effects of single-sex or coeducational schooling is perhaps the most volatile. As a 'debate' it re-surfaces regularly but with little resolution because, perhaps more than even most other educational subjects, it is prone to intense emotional feelings which override the pull or even the desire for evidence (Billig, 1989). Like popular racism it is a turbulent, polarized discourse where personal conviction rules. Many otherwise generally well-informed individuals insist that coeducation is good and progressive whilst single-sex schooling is bad and reactionary and will entertain no evidence which does not correspond with their own experience. Moreover, there is now a widening gap between public and professional opinion on this topic, with the public being nearly universally in favour of coeducation whilst a growing number of professional educationalists have returned to thinking well of single-sex education. This is quite a U-turn and largely the result of the introduction of league tables which consistently show how well single-sex schools do, particularly day schools for girls. Although undoubtedly flawed in many ways, the tables have at least put academic performance, rather than various aspects of the 'hidden curriculum', back at the top of the agenda.

The purpose of this chapter is not to review the evidence for or against either type of schooling but to look at how the debate has been conducted, what it illustrates about the processes of polarization around gender and sexuality in schooling, and at the unconscious elements and fantasies which underpin it. It argues that the deep structure of the debate is to serve as a defence mechanism which aims to suppress the subversive potential of sexuality. This angle allows us to see why the debate has remained controversial, why it is so polarized and why it is so resistant to rational discussion. Once it is seen as a discourse that serves a defensive purpose it is easier to see that it is not really about academic performance but about fears and fantasies which have become attached to schooling, sexuality, separation and merging.

My general point is not that fantasy alone is the *basis* for single-sex schooling (the British class system is far too important to ignore) but that different fantasies are embodied in the two types of schooling. The social anxieties which surround the debate are expressed by exaggerated claims for what each type of schooling can do for or to children, but these anxieties are themselves grounded in more primitive, individual anxieties. The fantasy/desire for fusion and equality which is embodied in the idea of coeducation has its roots in the infantile desire/fantasy for symbiosis with the mother, whilst the fear of parental sexual union underpins a good part of the support for single-sex schooling. Paradoxically, sexual separation is promoted both as a means of avoiding heterosexual union and developing control, and as a way of ensuring heterosexual object choice in the long run. Mixing is promoted as a way of avoiding homosexual union and of leapfrogging a stage in adolescent development. The dogged support for coeducation in the face of evidence that behaviour between the sexes in coeducational schools is not particularly harmonious amounts to a form of utopianism which has to be understood in terms of what it prevents us from thinking about.

The convention of generally educating the sexes together until puberty (end of primary school) and thereafter separately (secondary school) owes much to conscious fears of youth and adolescent sexuality, and is one of the starkest examples of how much organizational arrangements depend on visions of sexuality (Hearn and Parkin, 1987). But the unconscious role of sexual desire plays an even greater part. Roger Scruton, taking part in the Moral Maze on Radio Four (5 May 1994), explained his objection to coeducation on the grounds that it created expectations that it or society could not fulfil. He meant, I think, that society could and should not deliver social equality between the sexes, but his point can be taken at another level, to mean that coeducation rests on an unproblematic and idealized fantasy of union, which cannot be delivered. Fear and fantasy in almost equal parts have structured the form taken by British education more or less from its inception. Today it is a *return* to single-sex schooling which provokes a strong reaction. It is fears and fantasies about fundamentalism which constitute the 'risks' and supply the 'representations'. The detail is different, but the form is the same. Using sex as a dimension of organization is, in principle and in almost any context, defensive.

Social separation of all sorts feeds fantasy, which is why, in common-sense terms, coeducation is usually regarded as 'better' than single-sex schooling. It is widely assumed that if children of both sexes are educated together they will be more 'realistic' about each other and less prone to 'crushes', 'infatuations' and stereotyped or 'silly' behaviour. Yet fantasy is more complex or devious than this in its effects and institutions frequently operate in an opaque way. As Berger and Luckmann's (1967) classic account *The Social Construction of Reality* suggests, all social institutions are in some measure both created and sustained by the projections (or fantasies) of individuals. These projections accrete over time into institutions which then provide an emotional environment in which to generate, channel and/or reinforce emotional states in individuals. This is particularly the case for later generations who approach social institutions as if they were rock solid, rather than built out of layers of intersubjectivity. The same general point was made in chapter 3 in relation to Menzies Lyth's (1959) account of hospital organization and nurse training as a social defence mechanism, and is explored in greater detail in Mary Douglas' *How Institutions Think* (1987) which considers the social bases of cognition. Institutional solidity is often little more than projected fantasy and schools are no exception but in the case of single sex schooling and coeducation the debate is itself an institution in which the fantasy element is uppermost. The difficulties many have in even entertaining the idea that coeducation is not wholly progressive is closely tied to an idea/fantasy of heterosexual union and is reinforced by all the negative associations made in a homophobic society to any representation of homosexual union.

As this debate has become institutionalized as a polarized and defensive one, all who enter it are forced into a 'for' or 'against' mode and find it hard to argue, or to be heard to argue, for both types of schooling. The particularly volatile and emotive quality of this discourse has been amplified by the lack of good data, and perhaps at certain times by a determination to suppress data that would be useful. Although the DES (Department of Education and Science), now DFE (Department for Education) has routinely presented statistics about the performance of girls and boys, prior to the league tables it did not present them by type of schools and was unhelpful to researchers requesting data in this form. However, this has all changed since league tables which include private and state schools were introduced. Whether the tables are official or commissioned by various newspapers, the striking feature is the consistent high placing of single-sex schools, especially girls' schools and especially day schools. One can now talk about the subject seriously without having one's personal life or feminist politics assumed (i.e. not all supporters of single-sex schooling are radical feminists or frustrated old spinsters). However, the deeper issues which fired the debate and, for many years, shaped its discourse have not disappeared.

Background to the Single-Sex/Coeducation Debate

There is nothing educationally obvious about either single-sex or coeducational schooling; the reasons are largely historical. Britain stands out among European countries for its traditional stress on single-sex schools, especially boarding ones, which have become particularly potent symbols of the British class structure. In the middle of the nineteenth century, in England, when ideas of hierarchy and status were more or less consensual, the separation of girls and boys for schooling was unremarkable. Amongst the middle classes the ideology that boys and girls had separate educational needs was subscribed to both by feminists and non-feminists and the prevailing ethos was that respectability depended on sexual segregation. Pioneers of girls' education tended to conclude, pragmatically, that if girls were to get an education at all they had better go it alone, rather than battle for admission to the existing boys' schools. Hence the separate provision of boys' and girls' schools sprang more from a sense of what was feasible than what was desirable, though some of the pioneers thought that the two were the same. However, elementary education for working-class children was generally mixed and under one roof for reasons of economy, though fears of working-class sexuality and the need to 'elevate' children and teach modesty meant separate entrances, if not always separate rooms.

In class terms, the rationale for different schools for the sons of gentry, trade and workers was due to an amalgam of two contradictory beliefs. The first was that different classes had different intellectual capacities and occupational destinies and therefore *needed* different forms of education. To give them all the same education would simply be a waste of resources. The second was a fear of meritocracy and the subversive potential of education. In gender terms, it is fairly clear that whilst sex-segregated schooling had its origins in a belief and a socioeconomic system that saw little point in formally educating women, it was soon justified by an ideology that viewed girls and boys as intellectually different. The ideology 'took off' and, allied with sociobiological beliefs, was soon used to justify patriarchy.

Challenging existing gender relations is always a subversive act and the resistance it evokes is inevitably revealing. The opposition by boys' schools to the admission of girls, unless forced into it by economic circumstances, rested heavily on a broad range of fears, not all of which were explicit or clearly articulated. These were fears of contamination, fears of weakness and corruption, fears that masculinity and authority would be undermined or that the school's reputation would suffer, fears that pupils would be distracted, fears that lessons in hierarchy would not be learned if the natural subordinates (women) were afforded equal treatment in some sphere (education). Once associated with free thinkers and progressives there is no consistent political equation of coeducation with radicalism, or single-sex schooling with conservatism. Supporting single-sex schooling in the 1990s has its risks, including being stereotyped as a 'conservative' or a 'radical feminist', just as supporting coeducation did in the 1890s.

For all the optimism of the early feminists who thought that coeducation would reduce male dominance and open up opportunities previously denied to women, there is a companion, and reactionary, tradition of writers, usually men, who saw coeducation quite clearly in terms either of the benefits it could have for boys, or as a way of securing the traditional sexual division of labour. In the twentieth century, this line of argument is most forcefully represented by R. R. Dale (1969, 1971, 1974) who was keen that nothing should stand in the way of coeducation which he valued precisely because of the good social effect it had on boys and the 'happier marriages' he reported of the alumni of coeducational schools. But, as Carol Dyhouse (1984) shows, he had a forerunner in the Reverend Cecil Grant, who saw 'women as a sort of prophylactic for male vice'. As she points out, he was florid, but 'not far removed from mid-Victorian attitudes exemplified, for instance, in Ruskin's concept of women as repositories of spiritual virtue and moral guardians of the home'. Some supporters even saw coeducation as a way of combating feminism. Dyhouse traces the qualified support given by women teachers to coeducation and documents their fears (well founded as it turns out) that coeducation would impede women's promotion and employment prospects and lead to further attacks by male teachers. A flavour of the times is given by an attack made by a London County Councillor on the 'jaundiced spinsters' who wanted equal pay and were 'profiteers who took advantage of the war to extort money, which they had not earned, from the bitter necessities of other people', and thought that most men knew 'that women were made of an even baser clay than themselves'.

A similar trawl through the debates of the first quarter of the century led Kevin Brehony (1984) to conclude that Britain's first Professor of Education was right in perceiving the issue as being fundamentally about rivalry for power between men and women. Very rarely, as Brehony points out, did the cognitive outcomes of the schools feature in the debates. In some parts of Britain this rivalry culminated in a marriage bar for women teachers (Oram, 1989) which had, as its sole logic, the preservation of jobs for men. Even in areas where women teachers were not forced to quit their jobs on marriage there was often little support and much hostility, some of it actively orchestrated by trade unions as Margaret Littlewood (1985) shows in her study of the National Association of Schoolmasters in the 1930s. After the war, the sins were perhaps more of omission than commission, but women teachers continued to experience lack of support for their career ambitions (Davidson, 1985; Cunnison, 1989; Acker, 1989) and, with the drift towards coeducation, their prospects rapidly deteriorated.

Paradoxically, for a debate that has been so heated, when the moment arrived, the system of British secondary education changed from being predominantly single-sex to being predominantly coeducational with hardly a murmur of protest. Coeducation became the norm as a side effect of comprehensivization and owed more to the desire of local authorities to achieve economies of scale from larger, merged schools than to any belief in the educational benefits of mixed schooling (Weinberg, 1979). This largely unquestioned and unnoticed drift into coeducation was part of the post-war consensus about education and a generally 'Whiggish' belief in educational progress. By the end of the twentieth century, despite some local swings in and out of fashion, supporters of single-sex schooling had, in the public mind, settled into a minority position as extremists, subversives or cranks. However they viewed themselves, they were rarely seen as advocates of a practical and modest proposal to ensure that academic interests remained the primary ones in any discussion of schooling. The discourses of youth as a problem and of 'compulsory heterosexuality' (Rich, 1980) saw to that.

Separation as a Response to Fear of Femininity and Softness

For many years mothers, and indeed women in general, were regarded as a danger to young boys, and single-sex boarding schools became a means of separating them. All forms of femininity were equated with weakness, from which the apprentice ruling class had to be protected. The pre-war middle-class parents described in Christine Heward's *Making a Man of Him* (1988) accepted a class and gender code that denigrated mothers and all emotional warmth in favour of a value system of toughness in which only the fittest survived. Using letters from parents to the headmaster of Ellesmere College, Heward includes the sad examples of a mother who sent her son away because she 'did too much for him' and thought that 'he would make more headway away from me' and of the bereaved parents who were anxious that the head should not blame himself for their son's death, despite it clearly resulting from the harsh regime.

In the 1920s and 1930s, it was not only mothers who were perceived to be bad for boys, but women teachers too, a view that the militantly anti-feminist NAS teaching union was not slow to exploit. The problem was a general exposure to women. George Orwell, whose famous essay 'Such, such were the joys' (1968) includes a classic description of the pains taken by a prep school to corral and then distort all versions of feminine presence ends with Orwell's conviction that schools had improved immeasurably by the time that he wrote the essay (the late 1940s). Yet appearances can be deceptive, and neither Peter Lewis' (1991) nor Judith Okely's (1987) accounts of boarding schools in the 1950s and 1960s are substantially different. As late as the early 1970s, a matron in a boys' preparatory school was not allowed to be called by her name or even 'matron'; like all the other adults she had to be called 'Sir'. And right now, though a much gentler atmosphere is certainly promoted, women are still referred to in terms which make it clear that they have a time and place and need to be firmly contained.

Even in 1994, prospectuses for independent schools included such ambiguous claims as the one which assured parents that 'Routine medical attention is provided by a matron, a qualified and experienced nurse who lives in the Sanatorium'. The ambiguity in this centres as much on her restriction as on her availability. It was the only reference to a woman in the whole prospectus (for a coeducational prep school) which also explained that 'Regular social contacts are made with local girls' schools and frequent visits are arranged to theatres' – the two being somehow equated. Judging by a sample of prospectuses from schools in the south of England the commitment to coeducation is fairly superficial. It is striking how contained or minimal the female presence is in the independent schools which now admit girls, with mention of this restricted to one or two lines. Many maintain a tone and language of 'boys'-speak', though they also aim to assure parents that 'the presence of female staff, inside and outside the classroom, is of special value for creating a caring context in which boys can work, play and grow'. In prep schools the wives of teachers are mentioned and photographed to create an impression of a kindly atmosphere, but it is clearly tokenistic.

The analysis provided by Connell *et al.* (1982) that sexual divisions are maintained within and between elite educational institutions because they help drive home a broader message about hierarchy and offer some practical experience in leadership is robust. It is noticeable how heavily the rubric of the private school prospectuses still stress leadership – this is creeping in for girls' schools too, although the rhetorical emphasis there is more on fulfilment of potential and in this respect it is closer to the rhetoric of the coeducational state schools. Girls serve to give boys practice in leadership. Many of the punitive and humiliating practices of the older public schools were explicitly justified as part of this learning experience. If you are to mete out punishment, you must know what it feels like. The softer techniques of ruling, on the other hand, were better learned in other contexts and, as softer management techniques become more widely respected, the need for boys to acquire this experience through more contact with girls grows. But the general sociological point is that boys still have to learn about the legitimacy of hierarchy and difference and it is the independent schools' job to ensure that they do.

The Socio/Psychic Structures of Single-Sex and Coeducational Schools

The hold that institutions have on our ways of thinking can be profound and are essential for the continued existence of the institutions. As Isabel Menzies Lyth's (1959) nursing study suggests, even people who are deeply critical of an institution will go along with it if it serves their psychic needs. Both individuals and institutions find it hard to change, especially when personal and social dynamics converge. Something of this order might help explain why it is so widely assumed, without evidence, that single-sex education is reactionary whilst coeducation is progressive. If we follow Mary Douglas' (1987) argument that people cannot think beyond the institutionally given categories, this is not surprising, for the categories exist to maintain the institutions. Hence the florid 'life and death' tone of the debate about what might happen if the remaining women's Oxford Colleges went coed, because wild analogies and metaphors are devices for stabilizing fragile institutions. The more endangered the institution, argues Douglas, the more exotic the analogy or public discourse. There is then a parallel between the social and the psychological. At the individual level the more unconscious and primitive feelings are aroused, the more vehement the public behaviour and response. Such a pattern is clear in the debate about the types of schooling.

Douglas deploys Durkheim's distinction between mechanical and organic solidarity to explain why institutions rather than individuals make decisions and why communities are so often unable to be converted by reasoned argument. According to Durkheim a social structure based on 'mechanical' solidarity depended upon a low level of specialization and a high degree of publicly standardized ideas. Little individual variation could be tolerated. 'Organic' solidarity, by contrast, featured specialization and interdependence at the social level and led to greater independence for individuals (and to more identity crises). Though crude, this model offers a fair description of the respective social structures of single-sex and coeducational schools.

The principle behind single-sex schools is essentially that of mechanical solidarity, whilst that behind coeducational schools is of organic solidarity. Mixed schools demand interaction and rest on an ideology, or morality, that accepts difference, but promotes interdependence. (What happens is rather different and demonstrates how hard the theory is to achieve.) In terms of friendship networks and academic subject choice mixed schools often produce even more sex-stereotyped patterns than single-sex ones (DES, 1975). Many mixed schools are effectively unreconstructed boys' schools in which boys do not suffer academically, though girls do. This happens because the social structure of coeducational schools, whatever the intention, is more like the social structure of a single-sex boys' school and is based on a form of mechanical solidarity. The girls within it are still viewed as 'separate' and are related to as much through fantasy as are the semi-imprisoned pupils of single-sex boarding schools.

Literary Fantasies and Stereotypes of Teachers

Versions of these fantasies can be seen in the literary genre of the fictional 'school story' (Quigly, 1982; Auchmuty, 1992) and the long educational chapters in autobiographies and life histories (Coe, 1984). Early life and education are given much greater space and emphasis than later stages of life and the life history genre, though not uniquely 'English', has been developed and institutionalized to a far greater degree than in other countries and literary canons (Cockshut, 1974). The social and educational settings of the stories are usually far removed from the direct experience of most of their readers which gives rise to the interpretation that their appeal is based on displacement. Read by children of all classes, and especially by girls, they play on a series of contrasts between the readers' real lives and the escapist, timeless, parentless fantasies of the narrative (Frith, 1985; Rustin and Rustin, 1987; Rose, 1984). Elevated to a genre, they celebrate and secure the unattainability of the lifestyle. Even non-fictional memoirs such as Graham

Greene's (1934) collection *The Old School* or George Orwell's polemical 'Such, such were the joys' which were written as critiques have a similar effect.

Part of the appeal of this literature is that it is anti-teacher and draws heavily on caricature, especially of teachers in single-sex schools. Attacking female teachers as 'failures', because they were regarded as frustrated spinsters or lesbians, has a long history (Oram, 1989; Auchmuty, 1992) and is continued by more recent stereotypes of the married woman teacher as one who only works for 'pin money' and Jaeger coats. Winifred Holtby's heroine in *South Riding*, Sarah Burstall, is an exception (and a thinly disguised portrait of the head of Manchester Grammar School). In general, the female teacher is treated as fair game. They are usually portrayed as fuddy-duddy or half mad, as in Muriel Spark's *The Prime of Miss Jean Brodie* (whose male counterpart is probably the headmaster played by John Cleese in the film *Clockwise*). For women the images of teachers are of bizarre, obsessional, neurotics whilst men are either ineffective but lovable fools, or sadists. And, until Robin Williams played the charismatic teacher in the film the *Dead Poets Society*, there was no popular image of the teacher as a romantic hero.

This tendency towards caricature has a reason, though it is generally unconscious. It is always defensive and raises the question of what is it about teachers that is feared, or rather who is the teacher that is feared? The short and probably obvious answer is that teachers, like all adults, pose a sexual threat to children. The difficulty that societies have had in facing up to this phenomenon is well documented but it can also be seen in the polarized and stereotyped imagery of schoolteachers. Teachers, partly because they are substitute parents, are not meant to be sexual beings. The common caricatures of them therefore split feeling off from sex, very often equating the good teacher with the affable dedicated Mr Chips versus the sadistic, but sexually alive teachers at Lowood in Charlotte Bronte's *Jane Eyre*. Each caricature is an antidote to the other. Just as the brutal, sadistic teacher is a fantasy, so is the sexually harmless (impotent) and ineffectual one. Children can no more imagine their teachers having sex than they can their parents who, unconsciously, their teachers stand for. The caricatures that writers of children's fiction invent both express the fear and provide a means of defusing it by making the teachers harmless and unattractive.

Caricatures and Demonology: Muslim parents and Single-Sex Schools

A similar set of fictions, demons or caricatures appear whenever Muslim schools and Muslim parents' preference for single-sex schooling is raised. Publicly, both the main political parties have been slow to respond to demands for voluntary aided status for existing Muslim schools or the retention of single-sex girls' schools where they exist and, to date, all formal attempts to get voluntary aid status have failed. A few Labour MPs with large Muslim communities in their constituencies (Roy Hattersley, Ken Livingstone, Frank Field) have dared to support demands for Muslim education on the same basis as other denominations, but the more usual reaction from both parties has been to assert that Muslim schools, especially single-sex girls' ones, play into the hands of the 'fundamentalists' and consign girls to a feudal, patriarchal and oppressive regime. Little evidence is ever cited of what Muslim parents (many of whom are not fundamentalist) generally want for their children (Ashfar, 1989; Halstead, 1991; Parker-Jenkins, 1991; Haw, 1994), and the possibility that they might want single-sex schools for many of the same reasons as non-Muslims is almost totally ignored. The demonized caricature, or equation, of Islam with fundamentalism, with cruelty and sadism and, implicitly, with a form of oppressive and patriarchal sexuality is assumed. It is inaccurate and oversimplified, but it invites opponents of single-sex schools and of Muslim schools to view themselves as thoroughly progressive.

What is politically interesting and significant about this general reluctance to take the Muslim case seriously is not a rejection of woolly cultural relativism, but the unusual association of single-sex schooling with a non-elite group, especially one that challenges a notion of essential 'Englishness'. The denial of single-sex schooling to all but those who can pay for it amounts to its effective preservation for the upper middle classes. Single-sex schools were exempted from the 1975 Sex Discrimination Act largely because most of them would have been closed as illegal had they not been exempted. Clearly, financial considerations play a major part in this decision, but to have closed them would also have destroyed a major plank in the myth of essential 'Englishness'. Though very narrowly defined and based on an exclusive, aristocratic culture, not a national one (Eton, Harrow, or Winchester for boys, and Roedean or Cheltenham Ladies' College for girls), the single-sex, private, English boarding school symbolizes Englishness just as much as it does academic and social selection. By contrast, the coeducational school represents at least a partial commitment to equality of opportunity, to the desirability of social mixing and to the elimination of early selection. And, though its practice may fall short of the ideal, its social message is reformist.

When permission to survive as a single-sex school is given to selective grant-maintained schools but denied to ones with a Muslim catchment it is hard not to see connections between the value accorded to an elite form of schooling and fears of a growing and increasingly well organized Muslim population. Muslim parents are just as keen for their children to succeed academically as those who choose grant-maintained or private schools, so it is rather odd that they should not be allowed to achieve this through single-sex schooling if that is what they want. Part of the answer to this conundrum must lie in the confusion and antagonisms that surround Muslim claims to British citizenship. The equation of single-sex schools and Muslims with fundamentalism is clearly not rational though establishing the extent of this fear is difficult. There is little documented evidence in the realm of educational decision-making. Nevertheless, while the public grounds for refusing voluntary aided status to Muslim schools vary from claims that there is no demographic need to the perception that the applying school is inadequately resourced, hearsay evidence suggests that the decisions are driven by more blanket, less discriminating reasons. At the time of an ultimately abortive attempt to set up a City Technology College in Brighton – a project initiated and inspired by a group of parents whose children were nearing the end of their education in a primary Steiner school – discussion with the Secretary of State for Education ranged over the ground of how public the Steiner affiliation could be. The minister's unwillingness to be open about this was informally reported as that it would encourage similar Muslim applications.

As the locus of fear in Britain has shifted away from feminism or socialism and towards race, the fear that is most often expressed is of a 'rise' in Muslim fundamentalism. This takes many forms, especially in the wake of the fatwah placed on Salman Rushdie, but support for single-sex schools on the grounds that this is what a large number of Muslim parents want is invariably treated as a step in the fundamentalist direction (see Weldon, 1989). Yet, as so often happens when race, religion and gender are mixed up, it is not always clear what is feared most. In this case, is it Muslims getting assisted status and funds for their schools, or single-sex schools getting a new lease of life? Either way, the schools occupy a central symbolic position and justify the involvement of interests other than the local parents and, either way, the discourses are heavily infused with the language of danger and risk.

If a debate, especially an unresolved one, can function as a defence mechanism it is because it is a 'talking shop'; that is, something that avoids or contains action and whose role is essentially tactical. The next step is to ask whether it is action or knowledge that is resisted. There may be little difference, but I suspect the former. In the case of single-sex schooling the action that might follow from evidence that single-sex schools really do improve the academic performance of girls, or even of both sexes, could be extremely subversive. It is worth asking why, before league tables were introduced to simulate market mechanisms in education, the DFE wished to avoid making it easy to compare single-sex schools and coeducational schools? Could it have been to avoid any challenge to the general drift of educational thinking that favoured coeducation? Had questioning been allowed, and had it been well-informed, what might have followed? Might the cross-party reluctance to promote any educational reform that would increase expenditure (as a return to single-sex schools would) have been dented? Might Muslim campaigns to keep open some single-sex schools or get voluntary aided status for others have been helped?

These are difficult questions because there is no consistent equation between progressivism and radicalism and support for coeducation. Indeed, it is extremely odd that single-sex schools have not figured prominently in the Conservative attempt to turn the educational clock back. They have no place in a set of reforms designed to 'set the course of education into the next century' though, unofficially, through the grant-maintained schools scheme, they have made a remarkable comeback (by 1994, 30 per cent of all grant-maintained schools were single-sex as against only 13 per cent of LEA schools). Whilst most other aspects of traditional education have been explicitly reintroduced and viewed as the way of raising 'standards' this has not been the fate of single-sex schools, though their claims to do precisely that – to raise academic standards – are at least as strong as the current package of frequent testing, setting for academic subjects and a national curriculum.

More research would clearly make some people uncomfortable, from civil servants in the DFE or in LEAs, to the heads of private schools who have only recently gone coeducational. That local authorities are still closing single-sex schools suggests that the change currently most resisted is the preservation, or reintroduction, of single-sex schooling. Whilst information which would enrich the debate is not actively suppressed, it is piecemeal and hard to come by. Different strands of the politics of the issue have combined to render the subject near-untouchable. In toto, it is *as if* there was a diffuse reluctance to facilitate *informed* discussion in case it led to demands for action and change.

Ideologies of Sexuality and Schooling

The question then is to understand how, at different moments, single-sex or coeducational schools have become symbolically so important that their re-appearance or disappearance is seen to threaten the social order. This chapter has suggested that their capacity to unsettle is rooted in fears associated with heterosexuality in general and male sexuality in particular. The most common, prevailing notions of femininity and masculinity are based firmly and exclusively on heterosexual difference, a difference that has to be maintained. Ideologies of sexuality reflect this at all levels and sustain *both* single-sex and coeducational schools. What makes a nonsense of either arrangement is a notion of a fluid, flexible or polymorphous sexuality. Teachers and sociologists alike are quick to insist that it is gender rather than sex that we should be concerned with as gender is socially constructed and keeps alive the sense that change is possible. But all expressions of sex in schools cannot be naturalized as gender. Keeping the sexes apart may be justified either on the grounds that each sex has different needs or that sexual propriety demands it. Later on the case switches 180 degrees and in the twentieth century coeducation has been promoted on the grounds that each sex can and should benefit from contact with the other. Which ever way round the case is made the idea of sex differences is of something clear and unproblematic that can be manipulated. It was only when the ideas of sex differences and sexuality became recognized as various and variable that the rationale for either type of schooling falls apart, whether it is based on educational or sexual grounds. When this happened the debate about single sex or coeducational schooling assumed a different function – namely to contain a range of fears and provide 'solutions' to a sexuality that was increasingly seen as unstable and problematic.

Chapter 10

Conclusion: Gender Divisions in Future

The last chapter brought the arguments raised in this book back to the question of what, if any, policy recommendations are implied? Education is essentially a policy-oriented discipline and the question 'What should be done?' is always audible; whilst the answer, 'More research', is rarely acceptable, at least not on its own. However, the conclusion that more research needs to be done before effective policies can be pursued, especially around the issue of single-sex schooling and support for Muslim schools, cannot be avoided. It is odd, to say the least, for single-sex schooling to be supported in the private and grant-maintained sectors but not elsewhere. It is also a moment when the relationship between anxiety and educational performance could be effectively monitored and researched.

Although it would be myopic to think that every gender difference which occurs within an educational context is due to anxiety. I have tried to show how its effects resonate with social divisions of various sorts to consolidate gender divisions and gender identities. If there is indeed a relationship between anxiety and gender divisions within education it is because unconscious factors permeate the feelings and behaviour of teachers, pupils and parents alike, to the extent that we may add the unconscious curriculum to the well-known formal and hidden curricula. Because the anxiety-based curriculum is unconscious, the way it operates is devious and complex and, like the other two curricula, it both exploits and creates gender divisions.

Of course, gender divisions exist prior to any life experience which might lead someone to be anxious, just as anxiety clearly exists independent of gender divisions. The issue is how the two interact. That school tasks such as reading, writing, number work, computing, language learning, etc., produce gender-differentiated responses is uncontestable. What is harder to explain is why. The thesis of this book is that some part of these patterns are due to differences in emotional development of each sex, played out within a context or social system that is inherently polarizing and which fine-tunes itself by using anxiety almost as a form of energy. As each sex faces somewhat different crises, at somewhat different times, their responses to school-engineered crises differ too because, both socially and psychologically, the easy options, the defences, made available to each sex when faced with anxiety are different. If the thesis is right, it opens up a huge research agenda.

The British education system is moving towards extensive and regular testing. At the same time there is evidence that levels of anxiety amongst young people are growing (Rutter and Smith, 1995) and that adolescent anxieties are becoming more gendered (HEA, 1995). Britain is fortunate in having established a series of longitudinal cohort studies which include education and health data and have been running long enough for those interested to see if the educational and career decisions show a deepening of gender divisions in response to anxiety. This could be the next stage. So far I have simply tried to show that psychoanalytical ideas and the object relations approach in particular can illuminate gender divisions in the school context. They are not the be-all and end-all. As they evolve they are subject to intense and fierce criticism which fall outside of my range. However, because it starts from the experience of relationship, not of drive or instinct, and treats later behaviour as an elaboration of early experience, and because those entering school as children or teachers draw heavily on the parenting motif, object relations theory is a good way into thinking about school-based relations.

Whether children come from one-parent or two-parent families their experience of their parent(s) is never gender-neutral and forms the basis of the child's later understanding of gender; how schools receive, modify and elaborate this experience is, in turn, tied to the way it treats its teachers, male and female. As a consequence it is even more important to see teachers as emotionally 'in loco parentis' than it is to see them as legally taking on a quasi-parental responsibility. If schools allow and encourage teachers to labour alone and/or under the fantasy of the perfect mother/perfect teacher syndrome it is likely to drive teachers to rely on a series of defensive strategies which reinforce traditional sex stereotypes. All of this reduces the vitality of teachers' practice. Idealization, after all, is mainly a way of being self-punitive rather than of raising standards. It can deter teachers from applying for jobs because they think the standards they need to reach are too high and it can sap enthusiasm and lead to depression. The second reason for turning to object relations theory arose from Winnicott's idea of the transitional object and its application to more general cultural analysis. By seeing school subjects or disciplines as transitional objects we may understand how and why subject choice is polarized along sex-stereotyped lines.

I have tried to show how social structures or institutions respond organizationally to the dilemmas, tensions and difficulties associated with their central tasks by offering and embodying psychological defence mechanisms. These defence mechanisms, which constitute the unconscious curriculum, exist as organizational practices which are used both by individuals and collectivities. They are available to solve individual and organizational problems (or new and old anxieties) and will be resorted to the more the tasks that schools and colleges set their students revive or evoke memories of earlier fraught moments, especially those related to separation or to primitive fears and fantasies. In practical terms, relationships may be with teachers, parents, siblings, other pupils, the headmaster or headmistress, the school secretary, the groundsman and the dinner ladies. But they, and the unconscious curriculum, are driven by love and hate and by the experience of attachment and separation. Not all of these states can be reduced to fear and anxiety but they nevertheless comprise a good part of our prior experience and personal resources. They are what we bring to subsequent relationships and they lead pupils and teachers to get on with each other or not, to make friends, form groups, exclude particular people and fear or long for a change of class, teacher or school.

Like the other two curricula, the unconscious curriculum is a sorting and controlling device. It reduces tasks, orders chaos, eliminates aspects and people and confers a sense of control. It operates most effectively through defence mechanisms, both at the individual and organizational levels. It guides educational choices through unconscious identifications, first with people, then with the tasks which teachers invite pupils to do such as read, write, count, learn algebra, computing, a foreign language, etc. Gradually, for these school subjects take on the characteristics of people and become symbolizations of them. By extension, avoiding reading, writing, mathematics, etc. is closely tied up with avoiding something or someone which those tasks represent or remind one of. The case about anxiety rests also on recognizing that the feminization of the teaching profession has changed the emotional nature and character of the job by altering both the ideals of the 'good teacher', the 'good pupil' and the 'good parent' and the sorts of anxieties about their performance which afflict teachers of both sexes. Like any occupation, teaching offers those who enter it a chance to work out a range of inner preoccupations – they can displace activity, they can re-run past failures and they can create alternative identities.

The muddling of teaching and parenting is most evident in the unconscious links made between learning and feeding and most striking of all in the teaching of reading which remains, even in adult life, an activity strongly affected by unconscious factors. The argument about polarization and subjects, which in a way is at the heart of the book, applied Winnicott's idea of transitional objects or transitional phenomena to academic subjects and aimed to show how, as education progressed, academic subjects were treated organizationally as more important than people, although this was resisted by pupils who treated subjects as if they were still people. Most important of all, the personal element in subjects goes underground, becomes symbolic and unconscious, but retains its power to affect choice.

As schooling shifts from being person-based to being subject-based the equation of subject with person gets stronger. Thus the choice, polarization and sex-stereotyping of subjects is related to gender development, to the accommodations made respectively to the 'male wound' or the 'girls' crossroads'. The wound and crossroads theories (Hudson and Jacot and Brown and Gilligan respectively) each offer developmental reasons why subject choice is both fraught and progressively gendered, and each point to how the phenomenon most in need of explanation is the dynamic of polarization itself. Taking this focus lifts the problem beyond the individual and up to the group, the institution and the discourses which surround them. Classroom interaction and friendship groups based on gender need to be understood in their own terms, and not only in terms of how they meet individual needs. Similarly, the adversarial and long-running debate about single-sex and coeducational schooling needs to be understood as a defence against thinking about sexuality and about the sexuality of the young in particular.

In no sense is this anxiety thesis meant to be a comprehensive theory of gender and education, though it does suggest that several of the organizational problems faced by schools are the result of not attending closely enough to the experiences of teachers and pupils. In particular, the more administrators fear that the quality of teachers is declining and aim for more control and 'teacher-proof' methods, the more these methods infantilize and de-skill teachers, leading good ones to leave the profession. At the individual level teachers and pupils face different anxieties, but in each case their 'solutions' frequently reinforce gender divisions: boys retreat into gangs defined by their 'hardness' and denigration, whilst predominantly female teachers resort to idealization and the perfect teacher/perfect mother syndrome. The more unrealizable they find it to be, the more they denigrate themselves, feel trapped in teaching and lose vitality. As the British education system moves towards regular and frequent testing and the publication of league tables based on examination rather than 'value-added' results, it is very likely that sex differences of various sorts will become more apparent. If this happens they will need to be understood and explained. Already it is clear that not only do *girls' schools* do well in league tables but *girls* do well, as SATS results for the 7-year-old tests are beginning to show (See DES, 1991; Gipps and Murphy, 1994). This is a great opportunity to push forward on research into gender and education. We are in the position now, still fairly near the beginning of a new system, where we could measure anxiety in relation to tests and we could see whether performance levels and/or the depth of gender divisions, especially as measured by subject choice, increase as testing and the anticipation of it becomes a regular part of school life. We should look particularly closely at what happens when pupils are allowed a free choice and, if post-compulsory education is becoming the key area for gender divisions, this is where we should concentrate.

The currently improved educational performance of girls may, of course, be used to say that there is no longer a problem to be explained. This would be wrong; the problem of *how* gender affects educational performance remains, even if the specific focus of attention or 'underachievement' has shifted to boys. Much of the collective anxiety about Britain's poor educational performance, nearly always stoked by fears that in maths, science and technological subjects Britain lags far behind Germany, the Netherlands and Asian countries such as Japan and Korea (Prais, 1987) can be attributed to the depth of gender divisions in Britain in general and to its educational system in particular.

It would, of course, be a paradox if the testing that advances research on gender is also what creates the problem to be understood. But this dilemma has always accompanied social scientific research. Policy tends to demand simpler, more operationalizable solutions than researchers are generally wont to supply. However, policy options do flow from the relationship I have explored between gender divisions and anxiety. For if, as I have argued, boys and girls typically face different crises at different stages, then an educational system which does not take this into account but expects both sexes to proceed through the same system at the same rate may well contribute to covert discrimination. The impact of this may be amplified in educational systems such as Britain's which demand early specialization and in social systems, also such as Britain's, where social divisions are an important feature of social life in general. In countries where it is more common for students to carry on with their education well into their twenties, or even later, choices are less critical, less pressured and, because they are spread over a wider age range, less confused or mixed up with adolescent crises. Likewise, in countries where the 'A' level or its equivalent is broader, there is less demand to make an apparently irrevocable choice. But the timing and pressure of examinations for many pupils and students, in Britain, could hardly be more intense where early success or failure in school education can be viewed as final.

If we deny rather than understand gender differences, by taking the view that all we need in policy terms is to eliminate them, then we are likely to reinforce them. In Britain at the moment there is a crucial and largely misunderstood convergence between the educational and psychological life cycles which maintains high anxiety levels and deeper gender divisions than in many other countries. If the relationships between anxiety, gender and educational systems were truly understood then, as a nation, we might do much better, not just in making equal educational opportunities mean something real but in those areas where collective anxiety is growing such as the 'flight from science' and our poor grasp of foreign languages. In the short run it is fairly clear that we should also move swiftly to a broader 'A' level curriculum (along the lines recommended by the Higginson Report) and squash all discussion of two-year degrees.

Bibliography

ACKER, S. (Ed.) (1989) *Teacher, Gender and Careers*, Lewes, Falmer Press.

ACKER, S. (1995) 'Carry on Caring: The Work of Women Teachers', *British Journal of Sociology of Education*, Vol. 16, No. 1, pp. 1–36.

APTER, T. (1990) *Altered Loves: Mothers and Daughters during Adolescence*, New York, Ballantine.

ASHFAR, H. (1989) 'Education Hopes, Expectations and Achievements of Muslim Women in West Yorkshire', *Gender and Education*, Vol. 1, No. 3, pp. 261–72.

AUCHMUTY, R. (1992) *A World of Girls*, London, The Women's Press.

BARRETT, M. (1980) *Women's Oppression Today*, London, Verso.

BARRETT, M. (1992) 'Psychoanalysis and Feminism: A British Sociologists View: A Review Essay', *Signs*, Vol. 17, no 2, pp.455–66.

BARRS, M. (1984) 'Gender and Reading', *Language Matters*, No. 1, pp. 17–20.

BECHER, T. (1989) *Academic Tribes and Territories: Intellectual Enquiry and the Cultures of Disciplines*, Milton Keynes, SRHE/Open University Press.

BECK, U. (1992) *Risk Society: Towards a New Modernity*, London, Sage.

BERGER, P. and LUCKMANN, T. (1967) *The Social Construction of Reality*, London, Allen Lane.

BERNSTEIN, N., ELVIN, H.L. and PETERS, R.S. (1966) 'Ritual in Education', *Philosophical Transactions of the Royal Society of London*, 251 (772), pp. 424–36.

BEST, R. (1983) *We've All Got Scars: What Boys and Girls Learn in Elementary School*, Bloomington, Indiana University Press.

BETTELHEIM, B. (1978) *The Uses of Enchantment: The Meaning and Importance of Fairy Tales*, Harmondsworth, Penguin.

BETTELHEIM, B. (1982) *On Learning to Read: The Children's Fascination with Meaning*, London, Thames and Hudson.

BEVAN, J. and WEYMAN, C. (1989) *The Supply of Teachers: A National Model for the 1990s*, Report for the Association of Schoolmasters and Unions of Teachers/IMS Report 181, Falmer.

BILLIG, M. (1989) 'The Argumentative Nature of Holding Strong Views: A Case Study', *European Journal of Social Psychology*, Vol. 19, No. 3, pp. 203–23.

BION, W.R. (1961) *Experiences in Groups*, London, Tavistock.

BLACKMORE, J. (1993) '"In the Shadow of Men". The Historical Construction of Administration as a "Masculinist" Enterprise', in BLACKMORE, J. and KENWAY, J. (Eds) *Gender Matters in Educational Administration and Policy*, London, Falmer Press, pp. 27–48.

BLACKMORE, J. and KENWAY, J. (Eds) (1993) *Gender Matters in Educational Administration and Policy*, London, Falmer Press.

BOCOCK, R. (1976) *Freud and Modern Society: An Outline and Analysis of Freud's Sociology*, London, Nelson.

BONE, A. (1984) *Girls and Girls Only Schools: A Review of the Evidence*, Manchester, Equal Opportunities Commission.

BOURDIEU, P. (1971) 'Intellectual Field and Creative Project', in YOUNG, M.F.D. (Ed.) *Knowledge and Control: New Directions in the Sociology of Education*, London, Collier-Macmillan, pp. 161–88.

BOWLES, S. and GINTIS, H. (1976) *Schooling in Capitalist America; Educational Reform and the Contradictions of Economic Life*, London, Routledge and Kegan Paul.

BREHONY, K. (1984) 'Coeducation: Perspectives and Debates in the Early Twentieth Century', in DEEM, R. (Ed.) *Coeducational Reconsidered*, Milton Keynes, Open University Press, pp. 1–20.

BRENNAN, T. (1989) *Between Psychoanalysis and Feminism*, London, Routledge.

BROMLEY, H. (1993) 'At Last He's Looking at the Words', *Cambridge Journal of Education*, Vol. 23, No. 1.

BROWN, L. and GILLIGAN, C. (1992) *Meeting at the Crossroads: Women's Psychology and Girls' Development*, Cambridge, Mass., Harvard University Press.

BROWN, P. (1990) 'The Third Wave': Education and the Ideology of Parentocracy', *British Journal of Sociology of Education*, Vol. 11, No. 1, pp. 65–86.

BRUNER, J. (1990) *Acts of Meaning*, Cambridge, Mass., Harvard University Press.

BUCHANAN, J. and WEYMAN, C. (1989) *The Supply of Teachers: A National Model of the 1990's*, IMS/NAS/UWT IMS Report no. 181, Falmer.

BURGESS, A. (1990) 'Co-education – The Disadvantages for Schoolgirls', *Gender and Education*, Vol. 2, No. 1, pp. 91–5.

BURTON, L. (Ed.) (1988) *Girls into Maths Can Go*, London, Cassell.

BURTON, L. (Ed.) (1990) *Mathematics: An International Perspective*, London, Cassell.

BUXTON, L. (1981) *Do You Panic about Maths? Coping with Maths Anxiety*, London, Heinemann.

BYATT, A.S. (1992) 'Either a Borrower or a Lender Be'. *Guardian*, 2 March.

CAIRNS, E. *et al.* (1991) 'The Development of Psychological Wellbeing in Adolescents', *Journal of Child Psychology and Psychiatry*, Vol. 32, pp. 635–43.

CHISHOLM, L. and HOLLAND, J. (1986) 'Girls and Occupational Choice: Anti-Sexism in Action in a Curriculum Development Project', *British Journal of Sociology of Education*, Vol. 7, No. 4, pp. 353–66.

CHODOROW, N. (1978) *The Reproduction of Mothering*, Berkeley, University of California Press.

CHODOROW, N. and CONTRATTO, S. (1982) 'The Fantasy of the Perfect Mother', in THORNE, B. and YALOM, M. (Eds) *Rethinking the Family*, London, Longman, pp. 54–75.

CIOFFI, F. and BORGER, F. (Eds) (1970) *Explanations in the Behavioural Sciences*, Cambridge, Cambridge University Press.

CLARKE, R. (1988) 'Gestalt Therapy, Educational Processes and Personal Development', in PIMM, D. (Ed.) *Mathematics, Teachers and Children*, Milton Keynes, Open University Press, pp. 155–65.

CLARRICOATES, K. (1978) 'Dinosaurs in the Classroom – The Hidden Curriculum in Primary Schools', reprinted in ARNOT, M. and WEINER, G. (eds) (1987) *Gender and the Politics of Schooling*, London, Unwin Hyman/Open University.

COCKSHUT, A. (1974) *Truth to Life: The Art of Biography in the Nineteenth Century*, London, Collins.

COE, R. (1984) *When the Grass Was Taller*, New Haven, Yale University Press.

COHEN, D. (1990) *Being a Man*, London, Routledge.

COHEN, P. (1989) 'Reason, Racism and the Popular Monster', in RICHARDS, B. (Ed.) *Crises of the Self: Further Essays on Psychoanalysis and Politics*, London, Free Association Books, pp. 245–58.

COLE, M. and WALKER, S. (Eds) (1989) *Teaching and Stress*, Milton Keynes, Open University Press.

CONNELL, R.W. (1971) *The Child's Construction of Politics*, Melbourne, University of Melbourne Press.

CONNELL, R.W. et al. (1982) *Making the Difference: Families and Social Division*, Sydney, Allen and Unwin.

CONNELL, R.W. (1985) *Teacher's Work*, London, Allen and Unwin.

COSER, L. (1974) *Greedy Institutions*, London, Macmillan.

COULSON, M. (1972) 'Role: A Redundant Concept in Sociology? Some Educational Considerations', in JACKSON, J.A. (Ed.) *Role*, Cambridge, Cambridge University Press.

COWARD. R. (1992) *Our Treacherous Hearts: Why Women Let Men Get Their Way*, London, Faber.

CRAIB, I. (1989) *Psychoanalysis and Social Theory*, Brighton, Harvester Wheatsheaf.

CSIKSZENTMIHALYI, M. and ROCHBERG-HALTON, M. (1981) *The Meaning of Things: Domestic Symbols of the Self*, Cambridge, Cambridge University Press.

CUNNISON, S. (1989) *Making it in a Man's World*, Occasional Paper 1, Department of Sociology and Social Anthropology, University of Hull.

DALE, R.R. (1969) *Mixed or Single-Sex School? Vol. I: A Research Study in Pupil-Teacher Relationships*, London, Routledge and Kegan Paul.

DALE, R.R. (1971) *Mixed or Single-Sex School? Vol. II; Some Social Aspects*, London, Routledge and Kegan Paul.

DALE, R.R. (1974) *Mixed or Single-Sex School? Vol. III: Attainment, Attitudes and Overview*, London, Routledge and Kegan Paul.

DAVID, M. (1993) *Mothers and Education: Inside Out? Explaining Family-Education Policy and Experience*, Basingstoke, Macmillan.

DAVIDSON, H. (1985) 'Unfriendly Myths about Women Teachers', in WHYTE, J., DEEM, R., KANT, L. and CRUICKSHANK, M. (Eds) *Girl Friendly Schooling*, London, Methuen, pp. 191–208.

DAVIES, J. and BREMBER, I. (1993) 'Comics or Stories? Differences in the Reading Attitudes and Habits of Girls and Boys in Years, 2, 4 and 6', *Gender and Education*, Vol. 5, No. 3, pp. 305–20.

DAVIS, P. and HERSH, R. (1981) *The Mathematical Experience*, Brighton, Harvester Press.

DEAUX, K. (1977) 'Sex: A Perspective on the Attribution Process' in HARVEY, J.H. et al. (Eds) *New Directions in Attribution Research, Vol. I*, Chichester, Wiley, pp. 335–52.

DELAMONT, S. (1989) 'The Nun in the Toilet': Urban Legends and Educational Research', *Qualitative Studies in Education*, Vol. 2, No, 3, pp. 191–202.

DELAMONT, S. (1991) 'The HIT LIST and Other Horror Stories: Sex Roles and School Transfer', *Sociological Review*, Vol. 39, No,. 2, pp. 238–59.

DELAMONT, S. and GALTON, M. (1987) 'Anxieties and Anticipations' in POLLARD, A. (Ed.) *Children and their Primary Schools*, Lewes, Falmer Press.

DE LYON, H. and MIGNOULO, F. (Eds) (1989) *Women Teachers: Issues and Experiences*, Milton Keynes, Open University Press.

DES (1991) *Testing 7 Year Olds in 1991: Results of the National Curriculum Assessments in England*, London, HMSO.

DES (1975) *Curriculum Differences for Boys and Girls*, Education Survey No. 21, London, HMSO.

DOUGLAS, J.W.B., ROSS, J. and SIMPSON, S. (1968) *All Our Future*, London, Davies.

DOUGLAS, M. (1987) *How Institutions Think*, London, Routledge and Kegan Paul.

DOWRICK, S. and GRUNDBERG, S. (Eds) (1980) *Why Children?*, London, The Women's Press.

DURKHEIM, E. (1952)*Suicide: A Study in Sociology*, London, Routledge.

DURKHEIM, E. (1960) *The Division of Labour in Society*, New York, Free Press.

DYHOUSE, C. (1984) 'Feminism and the Debate over Coeducation and Single Sex Schooling:

Some Historical Perspectives', in Purvis, J. (Ed.) *The Education of Girls and Women*, London, History of Education Society, pp. 47–60.

Ehrenreich, B. (1990) *Fear of Falling: The Inner Life of the Middle Class*, New York, HarperCollins.

Ellwood, J. and Oke, M. (1987) 'Analytic Group Work in a Boys' Comprehensive', *Free Associations*, Vol. 8, April, pp. 34–57.

Erikson, E. (1968) *Identity: Youth and Crisis*, London, Faber and Faber.

Erikson, K. (1966) *Wayward Puritans: A Study in the Sociology of Deviance*, New York, Wiley.

Ernst, S. (1989) 'Gender and the Phantasy of Omnipotence: A Case Study of an Organisation', in Richards, B. (Ed.) *Crises of the Self: Further Essays on Psychoanalysis and Politics*, London, Free Association Books, pp. 101–112.

Etzioni, A. (1994) *The Parenting Deficit*, London, Demos.

Faraday, A. (1989) 'Lessoning Lesbians: Girls' Schools, Coeducation and Anti-Lesbianism Between the Wars', in Jones, C. and Mahony, P. (Eds) *Learning Our Lines: Sexuality and Social Control in Education*, London, The Women's Press.

Feingold, A. (1988) 'Cognitive Gender Differences are Disappearing', *American Psychologist*, February, pp. 95–103.

Figlio, K. (1988) 'Oral History and the Unconscious', *History Workshop Journal*, Autumn, pp. 120–31.

Frankenstein, M. (1989) *Relearning Mathematics: A Different Third R – Radical Math(s)*, London, Free Association Books.

French, J. and French, P. (1984) 'Gender Imbalances in the Primary Classroom: An Interactional Account', *Educational Research*, Vol. 26, No. 2, pp. 127–36.

Freud, A. (1931) *An Introduction to Psychoanalysis for Teachers*, London, Allen and Unwin.

Friedlander, K. (1958) 'Children's Books and their Function in Latency', *New Era in Home and School*, April, pp. 77–83.

Frith, G. (1985) 'The Time of Your Life': The Meaning of the School Story', in Steedman, C., Urwin, C. and Walkerdine, V. (Eds) *Language, Gender and Childhood*, London, Routledge and Kegan Paul, pp. 113–36.

Fromm, E. (1942) *The Fear of freedom*, London, Routledge.

Furlong, A. (1986) 'Schools and the Structure of Female Occupational Aspirations', *British Journal of Sociology of Education*, Vol. 7, No. 4, pp. 367–78.

Gambetta, D. (1987) *Did They Fall or Were They Pushed? Individual Decision Mechanisms in Education*, Cambridge, Cambridge University Press.

Gathorne-Hardy, J. (1977) *The Public School Phenomenon*, London, Hodder and Stoughton.

Gellner, E. (1985) *The Psychoanalytic Movement*, London, Paladin.

Gergen, K. (1991) *The Saturated Self: Dilemmas of Identity in Contemporary Life*, New York, Basic Books.

Gerth, H. and Mills, C.W. (1964) *Character and Social Structure*, London, Routledge and Kegan Paul.

Gilbert, P. (1990) 'Personal Growth or Critical Resistance' Self-Esteem in the English Curriculum', in Kenway, J. and Willis, S. (Eds) *Hearts and Minds: Self-Esteem and the Schooling of Girls*, London, Falmer Press.

Gilligan, C. (1982) *In Different Voice: Psychological Theory and Women's Development*, Cambridge, Mass., Harvard University Press.

Gilligan, C. (1991) 'Joining the Resistance: Psychology, Politics, Girls and Women', *Michigan Quarterly Review*, Vol. 29, No. 4, pp. 501–36.

Gipps, C. and Murphy, P. (1994) *A Fair Test? Assessment, Achievement and Equity*, Milton Keynes, Open University Press.

GOLDSTEIN, H. (1986) 'Gender Bias and Test Norms in Educational Selection', *Research Intelligence*, Vol. 23, pp. 122–6.

GOODSON, I. (1993) *School Subjects and Curricular Change: Studies in Curricular History*, London, Falmer Press.

GORMAN, T.P., WHITE, J., BROOKS, G., MACLURE, M. and KISPAL, A. (1988) *Language Performance in Schools: Review of APU Language Monitoring 1979–1983*, Department of Education and Science/Department of Education for Northern Ireland/Welsh Office, London, HMSO.

GRAY, J. (1976) *Teacher Decision Making and Reading Progress: A Sociological Study of the Teacher Effect and 'Good' Practice*, unpublished PhD thesis, University of Sussex.

GRAY, J., McPHERSON, A. and RAFFE, D. (1983) *Reconstructions of Secondary Education*, London, Routledge and Kegan Paul.

GREENE, G. (1934) *The Old School: Essays by Divers Hands*, London, Jonathan Cape.

GREENSON, R. (1968) 'Dis-Identifying From Mother: Its Special Importance for the Boy', *International Journal of Psychoanalysis*, Vol. 49, pp. 370–73.

GREGG, P. and MACHIN, S. (1993) *Is the Glass Ceiling Cracking? Gender Differential and Access to Promotion Among U.K. Executives*, National Institute of Economic and Social Research Discussion Paper no. 50.

GRIFFITHS, M. (1988) 'Strong Feelings about Computers', *Women's Studies International Forum*, Vol. 11, No. 2, pp. 145–54.

GRIFFITHS, V. (1992) *Wonderland: Girls and Girlhood, Transitions and Dilemmas*, University of Amsterdam.

GRIFFITHS, V. (1995) *Adolescent Girls and their Friends: A Feminist Ethnography*, Aldershot, Avebury.

GRUMET, M. (1988) *Bitter Milk: Women and Teaching*, Amherst, University of Massachusetts Press.

HALSTEAD, M. (1991 'Radical Feminism, Islam and the Single-Sex School Debate', *Gender and Education*, Vol. 3, No. 3, pp. 263–78.

HAMMERSLEY, M. (1985) 'From Ethnography to Theory: A Programme and Paradigm in the Sociology of Education', *Sociology*, Vol. 19, pp. 244–59.

HARDING, J. and SUTORIS, M. (1987) 'An Object-Relations Account of the Differential Involvement of Boys and Girls in Science and Technology', in KELLY, A. (Ed.) *Science for Girls?*, Milton Keynes, Open University Press.

HARGREAVES, A. (1986) *Two Cultures of Schooling: The Case of Middle Schools*, Lewes, Falmer Press.

HARGREAVES, D. (1967) *Social Relations in a Secondary School*, London, Routledge and Kegan Paul.

HARGREAVES, D.H. (1980) 'A Sociological Critique of Individualism in Education', *British Journal of Educational Studies*, Vol. 28, No. 3.

HARGREAVES, D. (1994) *The Mosaic of Learning*, London, Demos.

HARRISON, B.T. (1986) *Sarah's Letters: A Case Study of Shyness*, London, Bedford Way Papers no. 26.

HAUG, F. (1992) *Beyond Masochism*, London, Verso.

HAW, K. (1994) 'Muslim Girls' Schools – A Conflict of Interests?', *Gender and Education*, Vol. 6, N o. 1, pp. 63–76.

HEALTH EDUCATION AUTHORITY (1995) *Expectations for the Future: An Investigation into the Self Esteem of 13 and 14 year old Girls and Boys*, London.

HEARN, J. and PARKIN, P. (1987) *'Sex' at 'Work': The Power and Paradox of Organization Sexuality*, Brighton, Wheatsheaf.

HEARN, J., SHEPPARD, D., TANCRED-SHERIFF, P. and BURRELL, G. (1989) *The Sexuality of Organization*, London, Sage.

HERBERT, C. (1989) *Talking of Silence: The Sexual Harassment of Schoolgirls*, London, Falmer Press.

HEWARD, C. (1988) *Making a Man of Him: Parents and their Sons' Education at an English Public School*, 1929–1950, London, Routledge.

HEWITT, P. and LEACH, P. (1993) *Social Justice, Children and Families*, Commission on Social Justice/IPPR, Issues Paper 4, London, The Institute.

HILLMAN, M. (1993 *Children, Transport and the Quality of Life*, Research Report 716, London, Policy Studies Institute.

HINSHELWOOD, R. (1989) 'Social Possession of Identity', in RICHARDS, B. *Crises of the Self: Further Essays on Psychoanalysis and Politics*, London, Free Association Books.

HOCHSCHILD, A. (1983) *The Managed Heart: Commercialisation of Human Feeling*, Berkeley, University of California Press.

HOFSTEDE, G. (1980) *Culture's Consequences: International Differences in Work-related Values* Beverley Hills, Sage.

HOLMES, R. (1967) 'The University Seminar and the Primal Horde', *British Journal of Sociology*, Vol. 18, No. 2, June, pp. 135–50.

HORNER, M. (1974) 'Towards an Understanding of Achievement Related Conflict in Women', in STACEY, J. *et al.* (Eds) *And Jill Came Tumbling After: Sexism in American Education*, New York, Dell.

HOULE, C.O. (1984) *Patterns of Learning*, San Francisco, Jossey-Bass.

HUDSON, L. (1966) *Contrary Imaginations: A Psychological Study of the English Schoolboy*, London, Methuen.

HUDSON, L. (1972) *The Cult of the Fact*, London, Cape.

HUDSON, L. (1982) *Bodies of Knowledge: The Psychological Significance of The Nude in Art*, London, Weidenfeld and Nicholson.

HUDSON, L. and JACOT, B. (1991) *How Men Think: Intellect, Intimacy and the Erotic Imagination*, New Haven, Yale University Press.

HYDE, J. (1990) 'How Large Are Cognitive Gender Differences? A Meta-Analysis Using ω^2 and *d*', in NIELSEN J. MCCARL, (Ed.) *Feminist Research Methods: Exemplary Readings in the Social Sciences*, Boulder, Westview Press, pp. 207–23.

HYMAS, C. and COHEN, J. (1994) 'The Trouble with Boys', *Sunday Times*, 19 June.

ILLICH, I. (1971) *Deschooling Society*, London, Calder and Boyars.

ISAACS, S. (1930) *Intellectual Growth in Young Children*, London, Routledge.

JACKSON, P. (1968) *Life in Classrooms*, New York, Holt, Rinehart and Winston.

JAQUES, E. (1955) 'Social Systems as a Defence Against Persecutory and Depressive Anxiety', in KLEIN, M., HEIMANN, P. and MONEY-KYRLE, R.E. (Eds) *New Directions in Psycho-analysis*, London, Tavistock, pp. 478–98.

JAQUES, E. (1970) *Equitable Payment: A General Theory of Work, Differential Payment and Individual Progress*, 2nd Edn., London, Heinemann.

JONES, C. and MAHONY, C. (1989) *Learning Our Lines: Sexuality and Social Control in Education*, London, The Women's Press.

JORDAN, N. (1968) *Themes in Speculative Psychology*, London, Tavistock.

JOYCE, M. (1987) 'Being a Feminist Teacher', in LAWN, M. and GRACE, G. (Eds) *Teachers: The Culture and Politics of Work*, Lewes, Falmer Press.

JUDD, J. (1991) 'Are girls scared of exams: discuss', *Independent on Sunday*, 23 January.

KANT, L. (1985) 'A Question of Judgement', in WHYTE, J., DEEM, R., KANT, L. and CRUICKSHANK, M. (Eds) *Girl Friendly Schooling*, London, Methuen.

KANTER, R. (1977) *Men and Women of the Corporation*, New York, Basic Books.

KELLER, E.F. (1983) *A Feeling for the Organism: The Life and Work of Barbara McClintock*, San Francisco, Freeman.

KELLY, A. (1981) *The Missing Half: Girls and Science*, Manchester, Manchester University Press.

KELLY, A. (1985) 'The Construction of Masculine Science', *British Journal of the Sociology of Education*, Vol. 6, No. 2, pp. 133–54.

KELLY, A. (1987) *Science for Girls?*, Milton Keynes, Open University Press.

KELMAN, J. (1989) *A Disaffection*, London, Secker and Warburg.

KENWAY, J. and WILLIS, S. (Eds) (1990) *Hearts and Minds: Self-Esteem and the Schooling of Girls*, London, Falmer Press.

KLEIN, M. (1923) 'The Role of the School in the Libidinal Development of the Child', *International Journal of Psychoanalysis*, Vol. 9.

KRUSE, A-M. (1992) '... "We Have Learnt Not To Just Sit Back, Twiddle Our Thumbs and Let Them Take Over." Single-Sex Settings and the Development of a Pedagogy for Girls and a Pedagogy for Boys in Danish Schools'. *Gender and Education*, Vol. 4, Nos. 1/2, pp. 81–104.

KUHN, T.S. (1962) *The Structure of Scientific Revolutions*, Chicago, University of Chicago Press.

LACEY, C. (1970) *Hightown Grammar*, Manchester, Manchester University Press.

LAFRANCE M. (1991) 'School for Scandal: Different Educational Experiences for Females and Males', *Gender and Education*, Vol. 3, No. 1.

LASCH, C. (1977) *Haven in a Heartless World: The Family Besieged*, New York, Basic Books.

LASCH, C. (1979) *The Culture of Narcissism*, New York, Norton.

LASCH, C. (1981) 'The Freudian Left and Cultural Revolution', *New Left Review*, No. 129, Sept./Oct., pp. 23–4.

LEADER, Z. (1991 *Writer's Block*, Baltimore, Johns Hopkins Press.

LEED, E. (1980) '"Voice" and "Print": Master Symbols in the history of Communication', in WOODWARD, K. (Ed.) *The Myths of Information; Technology and Post Industrial Culture*, London, Routledge.

LEES, S. (1986) *Losing Out: Sexuality and Adolescent Girls*, London, Hutchinson.

LEES, S. (1993) *Sugar and Spice: Sexuality and Adolescent Girls*, Harmondsworth, Penguin.

LESKO, N. (1988) 'The Curriculum of the Body: Lessons from a Catholic High School', in ROMAN, L. and CHRISTIAN-SMITH, L. (Eds) *Becoming Feminine: The Politics of Popular Culture*, London, Falmer Press.

LEWIS, P. (1991) 'Mummy, Matron and the Maids', in ROPER, M. and TOSH, J. (Eds) *Manful Assertions: Masculinities in Britain since 1800*, London, Routledge and Kegan Paul.

LICHT, B. and DWECK, C. (1983) 'Sex Differences in Achievement Orientations: Consequences for Academic Choices and Attainments', in MARLAND, M. (Ed.) *Sex Differentiation and Schooling*, London, Heinemann.

LINDLEY, D. (1993) *This Rough Magic*, Westport, Bergin and Garvey.

LITTLEWOOD, M. (1985) 'Makers of Men: The Anti-Feminist Backlash of the NAS in the 1920s and 1930s', *Trouble and Strife*, No. 5, Spring, pp. 23–9.

LLOYD, B. and DUVEEN, G. (1992) *Gender Identities and Education: The Impact of Starting School*, New York, Harvester Wheatsheaf.

LOVEGROVE, G. and HALL, W. (1987) 'Where Have All the Girls Gone?' *University Computing*, Vol. 9, pp. 207–10.

LOWENSTEIN, S. (1980) 'The Passion and Challenge of Teaching', *Harvard Education Review*, Vol. 50, No. 1, pp. 1–12.

LYMAN, P. (1984) 'Reading, Writing and Word Processing: Towards a Phenomenology of the Computer Age', *Qualitative Sociology*, Vol. 7, No. 1/2, pp. 75–98.

LYND, R.S. and LYND, H.M. (1929) *Middletown: A Study in American Culture*, London, Harcourt.

LYND, R.S. and LYND, H.M. (1937) *Middletown in Transition: A Study in Cultural Conflicts*, London, Harcourt.

McCLELLAND, D. *et al.* (1953) *The Achievement Motive*, Appleton.

Bibliography

McCloskey, D. (1986) *The Rhetoric of Economics*, Brighton, Wheatsheaf Books.

McCrum, G. (1994) 'Sugar and Spice', *Education Guardian*, 12 July.

McGee, R. and Stanton, W.R. (1992) 'Sources of Distress among New Zealand Adolescents', *Journal of child Psychology and Psychiatry*, Vol. 33, pp. 999–1010.

McGuiness, D. (1985) *When Children Don't Learn: Understanding the Biology and Psychology of Learning Disabilities*, New York, Basic Books.

McIntyre, A. (1958) *The Unconscious: A Conceptual Analysis*, London, Routledge and Kegan Paul.

Mahony, P. (1985) *Schools for the Boys? Coeducation Re-assessed*, London, Hutchinson.

Marland, M. (1983a) *Sex Differentiation and Schooling*, London, Heinemann Educational Books.

Marland, M. (1983b) 'Staffing for Sexism', in Marland M. (Ed.) *Sex Differentiation and Schooling*, London, Heinemann Educational Books, pp. 42–59.

Martin, T. (1989) *The Strugglers*, Milton Keynes, Open University Press.

May, R. (1950) *The Meaning of Anxiety*, Ronald Press.

Measor, L. and Woods, P. (1984) *Changing Schools*, Milton Keynes, Open University Press.

Meltzer, D. (1973) *Sexual States of Mind*, Perthshire, Clunie Press.

Menzies Lyth, I. (1959) 'The Functioning of Social Systems as a Defence Against Anxiety: A Report on a Study of the Nursing Service of a General Hospital', *Human Relations*, Vol. 13, pp. 95–121.

Menzies Lyth, I. (1989) 'A Psychoanalytic Perspective on Social Institutions', in Menzies Lyth, I. *The Dynamics of the Social: Selected Essays*, Vol. 2, London, Free Association Books.

Milner, M. (1938) *The Human Problem in Schools*, London, Methuen.

Mitchell, J. (1974) *Psychoanalysis and Feminism*, Harmondsworth, Penguin.

Mitchell, J. (Ed.) (1986) *The Selected Melanie Klein*, Harmondsworth, Penguin.

Mitchell, J. and Rose, J. (1982) *Feminine Sexuality: Jaques Lacan and the Ecole Freudienne*, London, Macmillan.

Morgan, R. (1991 'In Defence of Single Sex Schools', *On the Map: The Magazine of the Girls' Schools Association*, No. 22, Summer.

Moss, G. (1989) *Un/Popular Fictions*, London, Virago.

National Commission on Education (1993) *Learning to Succeed: A Radical Look at Education Today and a Strategy for the Future*, Report of the Paul Hamlyn Foundation, London, Heinemann.

Nelson, J.S., Megill, A. and McCloskey, D.N. (Eds) (1987) *The Rhetoric of the Human Sciences: Language and argument in Scholarship and Public Affairs*, Madison, University of Wisconsin Press.

Nias, J. (1984) 'The Definition and Maintenance of Self in Primary Teaching', *British Journal of Sociology of Education*, Vol. 5, No. 3, pp. 267–80.

Nias, J. (1989) *Primary Teachers Talking: A Study of Teaching as Work*, London, Routledge.

Noddings, N. (1984) *Caring: A Feminine Approach to Ethics and Moral Education*, Berkeley, University of California Press.

Okley, J. (1987) 'Privileged Schooled and Finished: Boarding School Education for Girls', in Ardener, S. (Ed.) *Defining Females: The Nature of Women in Society*, London, Croom Helm.

Ollendick, T.H., King, N.H. and Yule, W. (Eds) (1994) *International Handbook of Phobic and Anxiety Disorders in Children and Adolescents*, New York, Plenum Press.

Oram, A. (1989) 'Serving Two Masters? The Introduction of a Marriage Bar in Teaching in the 1920s', in London Feminist History Group *The Sexual Dynamics of History*, London, Pluto.

Orwell, G. (1968) 'Such, Such Were the Joys', in *Collected Essays, Journalism and Letters of George Orwell*, Vol. IV (Eds Sonia Orwell and Ian Angus), *In Front of Your Nose 1945–50*, London, Secker and Warburg.

OSMONT, P. (1987) 'Girls, Boys and Reading', in Inner London Education Authority Equal Opportunities Team (Ed.) *Stop, Look and Listen: An Account of Girls' and Boys' Achievement in Reading and Mathematics in the Primary School*, London, ILEA.

OZGA, J. (1988) *Schoolwork: Approaches to the Labour Process of Teaching*, Milton Keynes, Open University Press.

PALEY, V.G. (1984) *Boys and Girls: Superheroes in the Doll Corner*, Chicago, University of Chicago Press.

PARKER-JENKINS, M. (1991) 'Muslim Matters: An Exploration of the Educational Needs of the Muslim Child', *New Community*, Vol. 10, no. 4.

PARKIN, F. (1979) *Marxism and Class Theory: A Bourgeois Critique*, London, Tavistock.

PARSONS, T. and BALES, R. (1964) *Social Structure and Personality*, Glencoe.

PENNAC, D. (1994) *Read Like a Novel*, London, Quartet Books.

PETERSEN, W. (1984) 'Age and Teacher's Role in the Institutional Setting', in DELAMONT, S. (Ed.) *Readings in Interaction in the Classroom*, London, Methuen.

PHILLIPS, A. (1988) *Winnicott*, London, Fontana.

PHILLIPS, A. (1993) *On Kissing, Tickling and Being Bored*, London, Faber.

PHILLIPS, P. (1990) *The Scientific Lady: A Social History of Women's Scientific Interests 1520–1918*, London, Weidenfeld.

POLANYI, L. (1985) *Telling the American Story: A Structural and Cultural Analysis of Conversational Storytelling*, Norwood, N.J., Ablex.

POLATNICK, M. (1984) 'Why Don't Men Rear Children?', in TREBILCOTT, J. (Ed.) *Mothering: Essays in Feminist Theory*, Totowa, N.J., Rowman and Allenheld.

PRAIS, S.T. (1987) 'Educating for Productivity: Comparisons of Japanese and English Schooling and Vocational Productivity', *National Institute Economic Review*, No. 119, Feb., pp. 40–56.

PRATT, J. (1984) 'The Attitudes of Teachers', in WHYTE, J., DEEM, R., KANT, L. and CRUICKSHANK, M. (Eds) *Girl Friendly Schooling*, London, Methuen.

PRATT, J., BLOOMFIELD, J. and SEALE, C. (1984) *Option Choice: A Question of Equal Opportunities*, Windsor, EOC/NFER-Nelson.

QUIGLY, I. (1982) *The Heirs of Tom Brown: The English School Story*, Oxford, Oxford University Press.

RAYMOND, J. (1986) *A Passion for Friends*, London, The Women's Press.

RAYNER, E. (1991) *The Independent Mind in British Psychoanalysis*, London, Free Association Books.

REDGROVE, P. and SHUTTLE, P. (1978) *The Wise Wound: Menstruation and Everywomen*, London, Gollancz.

RENSHAW, P. (1990) Self-Esteem Research and Equity Programs for Girls: A Reassessment', in KENWAY, J. and WILLIS, S. (Eds) *Hearts and Minds: Self-Esteem and the Schooling of Girls*, London, Falmer Press.

RICH, A. (1980) 'Compulsory Heterosexuality and Lesbian Existence', *Signs*, Vol. 5, No. 4, pp. 631–60; published as a pamphlet by Onlywomen Press (1981).

RICHARDS, B. (Ed.) (1984) *Capitalism and Infancy*, London, Free Association Books.

RICHARDS, B. (1989) *Crises of the Self: Further Essays on Psychoanalysis and Politics*, London, Free Association Books.

RICHARDS, B. (1995) *Disciplines of Delight*, London, Free Associations Press.

RICHARDSON, E. (1967) *The Environment of Learning*, London, Heinemann.

RICHARDSON, E. (1973) *The Teacher, the School and the Task of Management*, London, Heinemann.

RIDDELL, S. (1989) 'Pupils, Resistance and Gender Codes: A Study of Classroom Encounters' *Gender and Education*, Vol. 1, No. 2.

Bibliography

RIDDELL, S. (1992) *Gender and the Politics of the Curriculum*, London, Routledge.

RIESMAN, D., DENNY, R. and GLAZER, N. 1950) *The Lonely Crowd: A Study of the changing American*, New Haven, Yale University Press.

ROAZEN, P. (1970) *Brother Animal: The Story of Freud and Tausk*, Harmondsworth, Penguin.

ROBERTS, R., BRUNNER, E., WHITE, E. and MARMOT, M. (1993) 'Gender Differences in Occupational Mobility and Structure of Employment in the British Civil Service', *Social Science and Medicine*, Vol. 37, No. 12, pp. 1415–25.

ROSE, J. (1984) *The Case of Peter Pan: The Impossibility of Children's Fiction*, London, Macmillan.

ROSENTHAL, R. and JACOBSON, L. (1983) *Pygmalion in the Classroom: Teacher Expectations and Pupils' Intellectual Development*, New York, Irvington.

RUSTIN M. (1991) *The Good Society and the Inner World*, London, Verso.

RUSTIN M. and RUSTIN M. (1987) *Narratives of Love and Loss: Studies in Modern Children's Fiction*, London, Verso.

RUTTER, M. and SMITH, D.J. (1995) *Psychosocial Disorders in Young People: Time Trends and their Causes*, Chichester, Wiley.

SALZBERGER-WITTENBERG, I., HENRY, G. and OSBORNE, E. (1983) *The Emotional Experience of Learning and Teaching*, London, Routledge.

SAMUELS, A. (1993) *The 'Political Psyche*, London, Routledge.

SARASON, S., DAVIDSON, K., LIGHTHALL, F., WAITE, R. and RUEBUSH, B. (1960) *Anxiety in Elementary School Children: A Report of Research*, New York, Wiley.

SASSEN, G. (1980) 'Success Anxiety in Women: A Constructivist Interpretation of its Sources and its Significance', *Harvard Education Review*, Vol. 50, No. 1, pp. 13–24.

SAYERS, J. (1991) *Mothering Psychoanalysis: Helene Deutsch, Karen Horney, Anna Freud and Melanie Klein*, London, Hamilton.

SCANZONI, J.H. (1972) *Sexual Bargaining: Power Politics in the American Marriage*, Prentice-Hall.

SCHON, D. (1983) *The Reflective Practitioner: How Professionals Think in Action*, London, Temple Smith.

SEGAL, J. (1985) *Phantasy in Everyday Life: A Psychoanalytical Approach to Understanding Ourselves*, Harmondsworth, Penguin.

SEGAL, L. (1987) *Is the Future Female?*, London, Virago.

SEN, A. (1989) Gender and Cooperational Conflict' in TINKER, U. (Ed.) *Persistent Inequalities, Women and World Inequalities*, New York, Oxford University Press.

SEXTON, P. (1974) 'Schools are Emasculating our Boys', in STACEY, I., BERAUD, S. and DANIELS J. (Eds) *And Jill Came Tumbling After: Sexism in American Education*, New York, Dell.

SHAKESHAFT, C. (1987) *Women in Educational Administration*, Newbury Park, Sage.

SHAW, J. (1977) '"In Loco Parentis": A Relationship between Parent, State and Child, *Journal of Moral Education*, Vol. 6, No. 3, pp. 181–90.

SHILLING (1991) 'Social Space, Gender Inequalities and Educational Differentiation' *British Journal of Sociology of Education*, Vol. 12, No. 1, pp. 23–44.

SHILLING, C. (1992) 'Reconceptualising Structure and Agency in the Sociology of Education: Structuration Theory and Schooling', *British Journal of Sociology of Education*, Vol. 13, pp. 69–87.

SHUTTLEWORTH, A. (1985) 'Being a Parent', *Free Associations*, Vol. 1, No. 1, pp. 7–23.

SIMMEL G. (1909) 'The Metropolis and Mental Life'.

SIMON B. (1985) 'Why No Pedagogy?' in SIMON, B. *Does Education matter?*, London, Lawrence and Wishart.

SILVERSTONE, R. (1993) 'Television Ontological Security and the Transitional Object', *Media, Culture and Society*, Vol. 15, pp. 573–98.

SKIRROW, G. (1986) 'Hellisvision: An Analysis of Video Games', in McCABE, C. (ed.) *High

Theory/Low Culture: Analysing Popular Television and Film, Manchester, Manchester University Press, pp. 115–42.

SMITH, J. (1989) *Misogynies*, London, Faber and Faber.

SMITH, S. (1984) 'Single Sex Setting', in DEEM, R. (Ed.) *Co-education Reconsidered*, Milton Keynes, Open University Press.

SOMERVILLE, J. (1989) 'The Sexuality of Men and The Sociology of Gender', *Sociological Review*, Vol. 37, No. 2, pp. 275–86.

SPENDER, D. (1980) *Man-Made Language*, London, Routledge, Kegan Paul.

SPENDER D. (1981) 'Education: the Patriarchal Paradigm and the Responses to Feminism in SPENDER, D. (1981) (Ed.) *Men's Studies Modified: the Impact of Feminism in the Academic Disciplines*, Oxford, Pergamon Press.

SPENDER, D. and SARAH, E. (1980) *Learning to Lose: Sexism and Education*, London, The Women's Press.

STANLEY, J. (1986) 'Sex and the Quiet Schoolgirl', *British Journal of Sociology of Education*, Vol. 7, No. 3, pp. 275–86.

STEEDMAN, C. (1982) *The Tidy House*, London, Virago.

STEEDMAN, C. (1985) '"The Mother made Conscious". The Historical Development of a Primary School Pedagogy', *History Workshop Journal*, Vol. 20, pp. 149–63.

STEEDMAN, C. (1987) 'Prisonhouses', in LAWN, M. and GRACE, G. (Eds) *Teacher: The Culture and Politics of Work*, Lewes, Falmer Press.

STEEDMAN, J. (1983) *Examination Results in Mixed and Single Sex Schools: Findings from the National Child Development Study*, Manchester, Equal Opportunities Commission.

STRACHEY, J. (1930) Some Unconscious Factors in Reading', *International Journal of Psychoanalysis*, Vol. 11, pp. 322–31.

STROBER, M. and TYACK, D. (1980) 'Why Do Women Teach and Men Manage?: A Report on Research in Schools', *Signs*, Vol. 5, No. 3.

STORR, A. (1988) *The School of Genius*, London, André Deutsch.

SUTHERLAND, M. (1983) 'Anxiety, Aspirations and the Curriculum', in MARLAND, M. (Ed.) *Sex Differentiation and Schooling*, London, Heinemann Educational Books, pp. 167–83.

SUTHERLAND, M. (1985) 'Classroom Interaction and Sex Differences', in BENNETT, N. and DESFORGES, C. (Eds) *Recent Advances in Classroom Research*, Edinburgh, Scottish Academic Press.

SWANN, J. (1992) *Girls, Boys and Language*, Oxford, Blackwell.

TANN, S. (1981) 'Grouping and Group Work', in SIMON, B. and WILLCOCKS, J. (Eds) *Research and Practice in the Primary Classroom*, London, Routledge and Kegan Paul.

THOMAS, K. (1990) *Gender and Subject in Higher Education*, Buckingham, Society for Research in Higher Education/Open University Press.

THOMPSON, E.P. (1963) *The Making of the English Working Class*, London, Gollancz.

TONG, R. (1989) *Feminist Thought: A Comprehensive Introduction*, London, Unwin Hyman.

TOSH, J. and ROPER, M. (Eds) (1991) *Manful Assertions: Masculinities in Britain since 1800*, London, Routledge.

TREBILCOTT, J. (Ed.) (1984) *Mothering: Essays in Feminist Theory*, Totowa, N.J., Rowman and Allenheld.

TRILLING, L. (1961) *The Liberal Imagination*, Mercury Books.

TURKLE, S. (1980) Computer as Rorsach', *Society*, Vol. 17, pp. 15–23.

TURKLE, S. (1984) *The Second Self: Computers and the Human Spirit*, New York, Simon and Schuster.

TURKLE, S. (1988) 'Computational Reticence: Why Women Fear the Intimate Machine', in KRAMARAE, C. (Ed.) *Technology and Women's Voices*, London, Routledge and Kegan Paul.

TURNER, R. (1962) 'Role-Taking: Process versus Conformity' in ROSE, A. (Ed.) *Human*

Behaviour and Social Processes: An Interactionist Approach, London, Routledge and Kegan Paul, pp. 20–40.

TURNER, R. (1964) *The Social Context of Ambition: A Study of High School Seniors in Los Angeles*, Los Angeles, Chandler.

VIDICH, A. and STEIN, M. (eds) (1960) *Identity and Anxiety: Survival of the Person in Mass Society*, Free Press.

WALKER, J. (1988) 'The Way Men Act: Dominant and Subordinate Male Cultures in an Inner-City School', *British Journal of Sociology of Education*, Vol. 9, No. 1, pp. 3–18.

WALKERDINE, V. (1981) 'Sex, Power and Pedagogy', *Screen Education*, Vol. 38, Spring.

WALKERDINE, V. (1990) *Schoolgirl Fictions*, London, Verso.

WALKERDINE, V. and WALDEN, R. (1985) *Counting Girls Out*, London, Virago.

WALLER, W. (1932) *The Sociology of Teaching*, New York, Wiley.

WARNER, M. (1994) *Managing Monsters: Six myths of our time*, London, Vintage.

WEINBERG, A. (1979) 'Analysis of the Persistence of Single-Sex Secondary Schools in the English Education System', unpublished PhD thesis, University of Sussex.

WEINER, M. (1981) *English Culture and the Decline of the Industrial Spirit 1850–1980*, Harmondsworth, Penguin.

WEINREICH-HASTE, H. (1981) 'The Image of Science', in KELLY, A. (Ed.) *The Missing Half*, Manchester, Manchester University Press.

WELDON, F. (1989) *Sacred Cows*, Counterblast No. 4, London, Chatto and Windus.

WHITE, J. (1986) 'The Writing on the Wall: Beginning or End of a Girl's Career?' *Women's Studies International Forum*, Vol. 9, No. 5, pp. 561–74.

WHITE, J. (1990) 'On Literacy and Gender', in CARTER, R. (Ed.) *Knowledge about Language and the Curriculum*, London, Hodder and Stoughton.

WHITEHEAD, F. (1977) *Children and their Books*, London, Macmillan/Schools Council.

WHYTE, J., DEEM, R., KANT, K. and CRUICKSHANK, M. (Eds) (1985) *Girl Friendly Schooling*, London, Methuen.

WHYLD, J. (Ed.) (1983) *Sexism in the Curriculum*, London, Harper and Row.

WILKINSON, R. (1984) *American Tough: The Tough Guy Tradition and American Character*, Westport, Greenwood.

WILLIS, P. (1977) *Learning to Labour*, Farnborough, Saxon House.

WINNICOTT, D.W. (1953) 'Transitional Objects and Transitional Phenomena', *International Journal of Psychoanalysis*, Vol. 34, No., 2.

WINNICOTT, D.W. (1971)*Playing and Reality*, London, Tavistock.

WOODS, P. (1990) *Happiest Days? How Pupils Cope With School*, Lewes, Falmer Press.

WOOLF, K.M. (Ed.) (1950) *The Sociology of George Simwel*, Glencol, Free Press.

YOUNG, R. (1989) 'Transitional Phenomena Production and Consumption', in RICHARDS, B. (Ed.) *Crises of the Self: Further Essays on Psychoanalysis and Politics*, London, Free Association Books.

Index